Don't Fight the Process, PROCESS THE FIGHT

MARLON D. HESTER SR.

© Copyright 2024 – Marlon D. Hester Sr.

All rights reserved. This book is protected by the copyright laws of the United States of America. This book may not be copied or reprinted for commercial gain or profit. The use of short quotations or occasional page copying for personal, or group study is permitted and encouraged. Permission will be granted upon request. Unless otherwise identified, Scripture quotations are from the HOLY BIBLE, NEW INTERNATIONAL VERSION®, Copyright © 1973, 1978, 1984 International Bible Society. Used by permission of Zondervan. All rights reserved. Scripture quotations marked KJV are taken from the King James Version. Scripture quotations marked NASB are taken from the NEW AMERICAN STANDARD BIBLE®, Copyright © 1960, 1962, 1963, 1968, 1971, 1972, 1973, 1975, 1977, 1995 by The Lockman Foundation. Used by permission. Scripture quotations marked NKJV are taken from the New King James Version. Copyright © 1982 by Thomas Nelson, Inc. Used by permission. All rights reserved. Emphasis within Scripture quotations is the author's own. Please note that The House of David Publishing style capitalizes certain pronouns in Scripture that refer to the Father, Son, and Holy Spirit, and may differ from some publishers' styles. Take note that the name satan and related names are not capitalized. We choose not to acknowledge him, even to the point of violating grammatical rules.

ACKNOWLEDGEMENTS

To My Wife **Cheronda** *"Pretty Girl"* **Hester**
I would not have gained the momentum to write if it was not for the dedication, I have seen in you to write. Thank you for challenging me to be the best at being me.

To My Mother, **Karen** *"Lady Bug"* **Hoskins**
Thank you for supporting everything I have ever attempted to be successful at. You taught me how to love Jesus Christ and what serving Him is all about.

To My Children **Marlon Jr, Nieja, Mikel, Makayla, Meshauna, Anaiah & Ariyah** *I want all of you to know how much you have taught me. I have had the privilege of being a Father/Dad to some amazing, creative, gifted, and loving children. Always follow your dreams and stay with God through the entire journey.*

To My Sisters **Jolanda, Terri, Latrice, Berretta, Tanya & Tamara**
I really appreciate you guys for loving me and believing in me. You all have played major roles in my life, and I will forever be grateful for your amazing personalities.

To My Spiritual Parents **Dr. Rick & Carol Daniels**
Thank you, guys, for your leadership, guidance, and support. You guys have supported every idea, business plan/opportunity, conferences and have played a huge role in my spiritual maturity as a senior pastor. I love you guys dearly.

IN LOVING MERORY OF
My Beloved Brother **Juawaun D. Hester Sr.**
My Amazing Aunt **Monica Stamps**
Both were extremely instrumental in encouraging me in life.

ENDORSEMENTS

In the journey of life, we often find ourselves at the crossroads of conflict and resolution, struggle, and serenity. "Don't Fight the Process, Process the Fight" is more than just a book; it's a guiding light through the tumultuous storms we face, both within ourselves and in the world around us.

The essence of this book lies in its profound yet simple message: embracing the process is the key to transcending the fight. The chapters that follow are not just pages filled with words, but a series of steppingstones designed to navigate the complex dance of life's battles.

In these pages, you will find wisdom distilled from years of real-world experiences, insightful anecdotes, and transformative strategies. The author invites you on a journey of self-discovery, where each challenge becomes an opportunity for growth, and every conflict, a chance to learn and evolve.

This book is a testament to the power of perspective and the undeniable strength that lies in understanding and processing our battles. It urges you to look beyond the immediacy of conflict and to see the larger picture – the intricate process of growth and the ultimate triumph that awaits on the other side.

As you turn each page, I encourage you to reflect on your own life's struggles and victories. May you find solace in the knowledge that you are not alone in your journey and that every step, no matter how daunting, is a step towards a greater version of yourself.

Welcome to a transformative experience. Let's not fight the process but process the fight, together.

Apostle John Eckhardt
Impact Network Global

This book is a prophetic road map latent with wisdom from above. Apostle Marlon Hester has been graced by God to supply us with this powerful tool. He takes us deep into his personal journey and gives us an up-close encounter into a time of gross darkness and uncertainty. By God's grace and the guidance of Holy Spirit, he and his family have emerged victorious. My prayer is that you'll glean from the insights shared, gain a healthy perspective and embrace your process. I support this mandate and place my blessing on it!

Apostle Stephen A. Garner
Lead Pastor of Rivers and Chicago founder of Global Strategic Alliance Chicago, IL USA

CONTENTS

Introduction 7
1. Entering The Ring of Life 9
2. Decision Making 22
3. Pushing Through Pain 33
4. Valuable Nightmares 45
5. Birthing After the Breaking 57
6. Putting Things into Perspective 76
7. Choose Your Corner Wisely 87
8. A Warrior's Mentality 97
9. How to Win When You Have lost 109
10. Processing for the Future 129

INTRODUCTION

The catalyst for my decision to write this book is rooted in the many seasons where God has empowered me to reach the point of triumph.

Of all the competitive sports, boxing is amongst the most difficult. This contact sport is a blend of aggression and grace. We've seen some of the most amazing fighters dance around which gives the impression that it is an easy task. Boxing is an extremely difficult sport. I look at the sport of boxing as I do to live life. There are principles that must be used to be a fighter, a winner with hopes of becoming a champion and to understand ordained storms.

Life was never intended to be perfect, but rather it was bestowed upon us as a gift from a perfect God. He extends His grace and mercy to us during the less pleasant days. Walking by faith is the only way to gain a true perspective on the darkest moments we encounter. We have all experienced those days when it feels as though God is absent, until we shift our perspective.

I wrote this book with the intention of helping those who have faced shipwreck, lost hope, endured brokenness, betrayal, homelessness, sickness, consistent failures, and even those who have contemplated ending their lives. God has a way of preparing us for the new opportunities and spaces in life that we have prayed for. However, sometimes we are unprepared for the price we must pay to successfully attain those advancements.

This book will provide you with the principles necessary to overcome life's most challenging times. It is crucial that you learn how to embrace the process rather than fight against it. By doing so, you will be able to effectively navigate the fight called life.

CHAPTER 1
(Round 1)
ENTERING THE RING OF LIFE

Believe it or not, life is a part of God's divine plan for humanity, regardless of what may be taking place. He has predetermined our lives and given us free will to make our own decisions. We learn throughout life to put our trust back in Him to successfully live the life that He has predetermined. In contrast, some reject the notion of predestination, emphasizing free will and individual agency.

To understand the concept of being predestined we must also consider the fact that God is all knowing, and we are a part of His foreknowledge. God possesses knowledge of all things, including events that will occur in the future. God is omniscience, which means that God is all knowing. Therefore, God's foreknowledge implies that God has knowledge of every event that has happened, is happening, or will happen in the future. This includes the actions, choices and decisions made by individuals, as well as the outcomes and consequences of those actions.

God being all knowing does not do away with humanity having free will and determinism. The truth of the matter is that God has a desire to see us decide to do things aligned with His will, rather than our own. However, He gives us the freedom to choose.

With this understanding, we must begin to process life

to the point of first discovering who we are in God being that He knows all. This would also mean that God knows everything about you and me. It is extremely important to discover your identity in Him. God's idea of life concerning you is designed with a separate purpose that must be lived out by you. Only you can live God's idea concerning you because it is a unique idea.

Jeremiah the prophet struggled with discovering his identity for a few reasons.

> *"Before I formed you in the womb I knew you, before you were born I set you apart; I appointed you as a prophet to the nations."*
> **Jeremiah 1:5 NIV (*New International Version*)**

Like Jeremiah, God has foreknowledge of every individual, their life, and their purpose even before you are born. God has a divine plan for each of our lives and nothing happens by chance. Though you will have fights, obstacles and challenges God's plan will also utilize these experiences to make you better when you align yourself with His purpose.

> *"And we know that in all things God works for the good of those who love him, who have been called according to his purpose."*
> **Romans 8:28 NIV (*New International Version*)**

The most important decision you can make in life is deciding to discover and be who you were created and born to be. You were an amazing idea of God with a designated time to enter the ring called "LIFE." God has an expectation of you living your ordained purpose as a reality. Anytime you are not living God's idea of your life you are forfeiting your purpose in life. It is then that your fights, obstacles, and challenges will then work against you.

Being that life is so suspenseful, it is extremely important to discover your identity, develop your gifts, and talents while disciplining yourself to execute your purpose in the world to impact the lives that you have been assigned to.

Though life can take some serious turns we have the ability to sort through our daily obstacles by processing life. In order to have success in the ring of life, there are many tests we must pass. Life is not to be taken for granted. Neither should we become accustomed to wasting time.

Like the sport of boxing, you need to condition yourself to prepare for life's battles, obstacles, setbacks, and sometimes defeat. Though no one desires to feel or experience defeat, life has a way of introducing you to some of the most devastating experiences. Ultimately, we must process every choice and decision before making them to recover from disappointments. Many of these experiences causes you to sometimes ask, does God even care? The question is not does God care, the question to really ask is, have I humbled myself to receive God's care?

"Humble yourselves, therefore, under God's mighty hand, that he may lift you up in due time.
Cast all your anxiety on him because he cares for you."
1 Peter 5:6,7 NIV (*New International Version*)

It is crucial to always bear in mind that God possesses the ability to empower us when we seek strength. Nevertheless, it is possible that we may not appreciate the reality that God might orchestrate ordained obstacles to enhance our strength. Processing the fight of life is extremely important to become victorious. **DEFINITION OF PROCESS: Verb 1.** *Perform a series of mechanical or chemical operations on (something) to change or preserve it.*

In the sport of boxing, rigorous training is imperative to attain peak physical fitness and readiness for a bout, with the goal of triumphing over one's adversary. Similarly, in our pursuit of fulfilling our dreams, we ought to adopt a similar mindset. I firmly believe that individuals who emerge as champions in any sport, particularly boxing, cannot achieve victory without the guidance and refinement provided by competent coaches.

Life is filled with so many amazing experiences. Some of the experiences that make you cry are the most essential to maturing. Becoming the best version of yourself is going to require proper processing. You must have a readiness to fight through the pain and the anguish that may try to overtake you emotionally. Once you have discovered your purpose, there are a few methods that you can use to prepare yourself for some of life's greatest challenges. It is extremely difficult to process life without following principles and trustworthy instructions.

Take for instance a boxer, he or she is instructed to do certain things before getting into a ring to fight his opponents. The great Floyd **Mayweather Jr.** said, *"You* *have some fighters who are better skilled fighters than others. These are those who are more naturally talented and may even hit harder. Then you have the fighter that puts in all the hard training, does his daily runs, and works hard. That fighter's evidence will show up in the ring better than the naturally skilled fighter. Speed and power do not win fights, but those who outsmart their opponent by utilizing their training wins."*

It is the same in life. You must utilize what you have learned from mistakes to be successful at processing for future endeavors. Life can be lived victoriously regardless of your present or past pains. You can win this fight. It is actually fixed and working in your favor when you discover the purpose that God has already ordained.

*And we know that in **all things God works for the good of those who love him**, who[i] have been called according to his purpose. For those God **foreknew** he also **predestined** to be conformed to the image of his Son, that he might be the firstborn among many brothers and sisters. And those he **predestined**, he also called; those he called, he also justified; those he justified, he also glorified.*

Romans 8:28 - 30 NIV (New International Version)

Sometimes your experiences can overwhelm you and challenge your faith, but you must remember the scriptures and declare them over your life. I am writing this portion of this book right now with vision lost in my left eye. Yet I believe the book must be written to help people like you press through. I hope that my transparency helps you not only to find strength but to also become victorious in your entire life.

I was born with a sickle cell blood disease that plagued my life along with my brother who has now gone home to be with the Lord. The age of 6 was the first time I was aware of a sickle cell pain crisis. My Brother and I were given until the age of twenty-two to live because of this disease. Our Mother was told that our spleens would have to be removed by the age of twelve, and we would not stand past five foot seven. On March 21, 2024, I turned Fifty, I now weigh two hundred and forty pounds and I still have a spleen today while standing six foot one. I give all the glory to God for gifting us with a praying Mother, my identity in Him and the determination to press beyond the negatives that were spoken against us early on in life.

Today is December 2, 2024, and I am writing with blurred vision in my left eye because of this disease. However, I am victorious despite the fact that I still have life, breath, and strength along with a healthy family. I am processing through this challenge by remembering the truths that I have studied from the Word of God.

For our light and momentary troubles are achieving for us an eternal glory that far outweighs them all.

1 Corinthians 4:17 NIV (New International Version)

- *Agree with God that your afflictions are light (regardless of how you feel).*

- *Agree with God that your afflictions are momentary.*

- *Believe the word of God and overpower your emotions with the truth of God's word.*

This requires a prayer life and a committed walk of faith because the truth of the matter is, you may be going through some very difficult things and can hardly relax your mind. I have been there. I know the feeling of casting the devil out of others and living with the same anxiety that I just saw leave the person I was praying for. I am not encouraging you to pretend but I am challenging you to believe God through it all!

Below are a few principles to live by as we continue processing this journey called "*The Fight of Life.*" Let us look at the life of Job as an example:

*And the LORD said unto Satan, Hast thou **considered** my servant Job, that there is none like him in the earth, a perfect and an upright man, **one that feareth God**, and escheweth (depart) evil?*
Job 1:8

Principle #1: *Embrace the life that God has already predestined for you. He chose your path which also includes obstacles that will make you stronger along the way. We must remember that satan considers us with hopes that we will turn against God. Learn to love God through it all.*

Looking through the lenses of God is extremely important when it comes to staying the course during challenging times in life. Our faith combined with my mother's faith in God is how we made it through life. When your life is ordained and orchestrated by God, the obstacles can and will only make you stronger. Because of this mindset, I have carried others with a passion. I look forward to seeing miracles in their lives just as God has allowed me to see in my own.

And the LORD said unto Satan, Behold, all that he hath is in thy power; only upon himself put not forth thine hand. So Satan went forth from the presence of the LORD.
Job 1:12

Principle #2: *Satan can only bother you by way of permission that God gives. Trust in God not your own emotions. When all of your trust is in God it causes God to back you up 100 %.*

There are times when we bring certain things on ourselves, but then there are things we go through because God has permitted satan to try you to make a fool out of him instead of him making a fool out of you. It is at this point that you realize the importance of aligning yourself with God's plan and not your own desires. It is especially when you're executing the path of righteousness that satan considers you as an attack with hopes of getting you off track and out of alignment with God. Don't allow your emotions to overtake you. I know this may be difficult to accomplish. I have been there, but I have also experienced everything I am sharing with you, and it works!

Learning to express yourself emotionally is essential to carry your purpose in life. Like a pregnant woman who must learn her body, deal with the changes, and outgrowing her environment from one month to the next is the same way you must cater to your own emotions while in the place of prayer with fasting to not abort. Job put all his trust in the Lord when all odds were against him.

Then Job arose, and rent his mantle, and shaved his head, and fell down upon the ground, and worshipped,
Job 1:20

You may have external expressions of going through and being weak during your fight but always remember to respond to God properly through it all. Job got up, tore his robe as a sign of grief and distress. He then shaved his head. Job did all of this to demonstrate his pain after losing all that he owned including losing his children. He was walking out the path of fearing God and shunning evil at the same time.

Many have given up because of the lack of endurance. Some don't have the ability to deal with pain productively because of their lack of a relationship with God. The lack thereof causes you to lose the grip of what can potentially happen in your future. You must endure and hold on to the future that God has for you.

Job had to believe in the same God who gave satan permission to attack him. Our relationship with God is not natural but rather spiritual. God has full control of what happens to us naturally by the way we respond to him spiritually. Being spiritually connected is extremely important to live through some of the worst situations in life. After Job tore his robe, shaved his head to express his emotions, he chose to worship overall.

Principle #3: *You may have to face some things that can't be changed but you can only change things when you attempt to face them head on.*

Like Job we will have to make this conscious decision. God giveth and God taketh away. You win some and you win some more! As long as it is God in control you are always going to win. There is absolutely no failure in God.

Even in the sport of boxing the fighter has to give up food, sleep, fun and even time with family sometimes to win the fight. The key to boxing is not to get hit but every fighter prepares for the day that may be a bit more physical than others. You must prepare for the pain.

You don't win the fight in the ring. You win the fight in the gym working out, riding the bike, jumping rope, sparring with other great fighters and still…. This is only preparation. You still must get in the ring to fight the real fight.

All my victorious moments came after deciding to trust God and face my fears, challenges, and enemies of my destiny. Your mind must be conditioned to believe that you will never lose when you are trusting in God and His promises. It is not always comfortable, but God is always dependable.

Redefining fear is extremely important if you are going to fight your way through certain seasons and challenges. There are certain seasons that are more difficult than others yet still rewarding even after all the pain. Fight your way through. Face your fears and you will experience your victories regardless of how many times you may get knocked down. Have the mindset of Job. He lost his children, property, friends and his wife and Job still responded soberly concerning God:

And said, Naked came I out of my mother's womb, and naked shall I return thither: the LORD gave, and the LORD hath taken away; **blessed be the name of the LORD**. *In all this Job sinned not, nor charged God foolishly.*
Job 1:22

Christ saw defeat in His cup of life, but He still decided to drink from it to please His Father. There will be times in life when you will have to drink bitter cups to please God. Putting all your trust in God during those difficult times are extremely important to come out victorious. Christ was innocent and wrongly charged but His response was:

"My Father! If it is possible, let this cup of suffering be taken away from me. Yet I want your will to be done, not mine."
Matthew 26:39 NLT (New Living Translation)

A mindset to win is the only way to enter each season of life. Agreeing with the will of God regardless of whether times are easy or times get hard, you must decide that winning is the only option especially if others are depending on you. Winning is not always easy. Most memorable wins will be won with a good fight. It takes faith to win fights that are ahead of you that you are not aware of. The plan of God is perfect but filled with surprises. There were many great people in the Bible who fought with faith and won.

1. **John the Baptist:** John who was sent to prepare the way of the Lord started out confident. When talking about Jesus, he said, *"Look, the Lamb of God, who takes away the sin of the world! And, I have seen and I testify that this is God's Chosen One."* But when he was put in prison, he questioned if Jesus was really the Messiah. John sent his disciples to ask Jesus if he was *the one*.

2. **Simon Peter:** In addition to the original twelve disciples of Jesus, Peter is renowned for his courage. Jesus commended Peter for receiving the revelation from the Father that Jesus was the Son of the Living God. However, when Jesus was arrested, Peter struggled with a conflict between faith and fear. He went as far as denying any knowledge of Jesus and even using profane language. Peter had previously been confident in his faith, but Jesus knew that he truly wasn't. Jesus had already foretold Peter's denial and prayed for his faith not to falter — and it didn't. Peter's faith ultimately led him back to Jesus, who not only reconciled with him but also entrusted him with the task of shepherding His followers.

3. **Father of a Son with A Dumb and Deaf Spirit:** Here is a father with a son who's mute and battling epilepsy. He takes his son to the disciples of Jesus to be healed and they were unsuccessful. Fighting to process his faith, he brings his son to Jesus asking

if Jesus could help. Jesus points to his faith.

4. But knowing he's wrestling with his faith; the father responds honestly. "I **believe, help mine unbelief**," and Jesus brought the victory. God will help you process the fight by faith and by His **grace**.

5. **Moses:** Moses being one of the most prominent figures in the Bible endured many rounds. He fought with **faith** struggling to believe he could be Israel's Deliverer after murdering an Egyptian and being rejected by his Hebrew brothers. After this, he ran into the wilderness where the Lord appeared to him in the burning bush. But when God called him, he fought with his faith with questions like, *what if they don't believe me or listen to me?* Every fight with faith that Moses went through was met by processing the fight with faith and with the grace of God.

CHAPTER 2
(Round 2)
DECISION MAKING

Decision making is the process of choosing a course of action from among multiple alternatives. It is a critical skill in both personal and professional contexts, as individuals and organizations are constantly faced with choices that can have significant consequences.

There are various approaches to decision making, and different techniques may be more appropriate depending on the specific situation. Some common approaches to decision making include:

1. **Rational decision making:** This approach involves systematically analyzing the available information, identifying the options, and evaluating them based on predefined criteria. The goal is to make an optimal decision based on logic and reasoning.

2. **Intuitive decision making:** Intuition involves making decisions based on a *"gut feeling"* or instinct, often drawing on past experiences and implicit knowledge. While it can be effective in certain situations, intuitive decision making can also be influenced by biases and emotions.

3. **Decision making under uncertainty:** In situations where there is incomplete or ambiguous information, decision makers must assess the likelihood of different outcomes and consider the potential risks and benefits associated with each option.

4. **Collaborative decision making:** In many contexts, decision making involves managing the dynamics of teamwork, incorporating divers perspectives, and reaching consensus among team members.

5. **Decision making with ethical considerations:** Ethical decision making involves considering the moral implications of choices and striving to make decisions that align with principles of fairness, integrity, and social responsibility.

6. **Spiritual decision making:** This form of decision making involves incorporating spiritual principles, values, and beliefs into the process of making choices. For individuals who are guided by their spirituality or religious beliefs, decision making is not purely a rational or logical process, but also a deeply personal and often moral or ethical one.

Effective decision making often involves a combination of these approaches, as well as an awareness of potential cognitive biases and emotional influences that can impact the decision-making process. Ultimately, good decision making requires critical thinking, sound judgement, and the ability to weigh the potential outcomes of different choices to make informed and effective decisions.

I have chosen to be more spiritual in processing my decisions since I am responsible for leading an integral life and looked upon as one who portrays godly morals partnered with a standard of living. I depend on God's Holy Spirit and His Wisdom which leads me into making decisions that will glorify His truths instead of highlighting my emotions. You must ask God for His wisdom because He gives it to us generously without finding fault in us. He knows we have made many decisions without His wisdom. God desires to give His divine wisdom to His children.

If any of you lacks wisdom, you should ask God, who gives generously to all without finding fault, and it will be given to you.
James 1:5 NIV (New International Version)

It should be everyone's desire to be wise to live a productive life. Also, so that we can hone the ability to answer questions, to make decisions, and to share what we know with one another. We must search for wisdom and knowledge of the things of this world, just as Solomon did. However, Solomon discovered that wisdom 'under the sun', apart from God, left him unfulfilled and discontented.

Then I applied myself to the understanding of wisdom, and also of madness and folly, but I learned that this, too, is a chasing after the wind.
Ecclesiastes 1:17 NIV (New International Version)

Earthly wisdom appeals to the senses and the emotions. In contrast, the wisdom that is from God reflects Him.

- While earthly wisdom says always follow your heart, godly wisdom tells us in **Jeremiah 17:9** that *"the heart is deceitful above all things."*
- While earthly wisdom says seeing is believing, godly wisdom tells us in **John 20:29** that *"blessed are those who have not seen and yet have believed."*

- While earthly wisdom says love your family and friends, godly wisdom tells us in **Matthew 5:43-47** to also *"love your enemies and bless them."*
- While earthly wisdom says there are many ways to God, godly wisdom tells us in **Acts 4:12** *"there is only one way to God, Jesus Christ."*

The guidance of the Spirit of God, coupled with His wisdom, provides us with clarity and purpose when we are faced with the choice between what appears good, what feels good, and what truly is good. It is important to recognize that not everything that seems good aligns with God's will.

There are certain phases in life during which we need to rely on God's wisdom, adhere to the right processes, and make disciplined decisions. The period between 2019 and 2023 was particularly challenging for me, as I found myself grappling with life's struggles more intensely than ever before. It was a season of decisions that significantly impacted my future, as well as the stability of my family, church community, and ministry partners.

In February of 2020, during my time of prayer, I distinctly heard the Lord instructing me to resume hosting our weekly church services virtually online. This initiative had originally begun in the year 2000, with the simple aim of reaching people worldwide. What had initially started as a chat room unexpectedly evolved into a local church in 2006, following the Lord's guidance to plant Greater Works Ministries International.

In February 2020, we heeded the divine call and

resumed our services virtually, faithfully following the voice of the Lord. Little did we know that by March 2020, the world would be forever altered by the onset of the pandemic. It was an unprecedented and perilous time; unlike anything we could have ever imagined. I am grateful that we had already chosen to prioritize God's guidance over our own desires to persist with in-person gatherings. This choice can be regarded as a spiritual decision, guided by our faith. This decision can be categorized as an example of **spiritual decision making.**

The initial significant decision I had to make April 5, 2021, was whether to leave a rented house or buy a new one. Among the crucial factors to consider were the closing procedure and the timeframe for completion. I was collaborating with an individual who made numerous empty commitments and I relied on his assurances.

Filled with enthusiasm and having a stable financial situation, I opted to temporarily reside in a hotel after he presented us with an apparently favorable opportunity. This particular decision can be categorized as an example of **decision making under uncertainty.**

During our initial week at the hotel, I unfortunately contracted Covid, and my children also fell ill. The severity of the situation became apparent when I nearly lost my life to the virus. It was truly unbelievable that while in the midst of making one of the most crucial decisions in my life, I was suddenly confronted with the possibility of losing it. Realizing the urgency to acquire a home, I understood the importance of carefully selecting the right person to assist me in achieving this objective. I made the decision to part ways with the individual who made empty promises.

Before checking into the hotel, we had already spent months providing all the necessary information to secure a place at the table and finalize the purchase of our home. We were under the impression that once we moved into the hotel, it would only take 7 more days to reach the closing point. We were recommended to someone else who was known for helping families as a mortgage loan originator. He ended up informing us that the closing process would take a bit longer. As a result, our stay at the hotel extended to a grueling 4 months. These 4 months were filled with unhealthy eating, incredibly stressful days, and an emotionally challenging journey as my wife and I embarked on purchasing our very first home together. This decision could have been categorized as an example of **rational decision making.**

This journey I embarked upon proved to be one of the most excruciating ordeals I had ever encountered in my life. It felt as if our very survival was hanging in the balance. I had to acquire the skill of navigating through the obstacles without resisting the process itself. Each passing day presented us with fresh lessons that we had to grasp. The level of stress, invasion of privacy, and demoralization that accompanied the home-buying process exceeded my expectations. Nevertheless, I had to confront reality and admit that it was my own decisions that led us to this predicament. I was determined to strive to make wiser decisions and find a way to extricate ourselves from this situation.

Consequently, I had to resort to **intuitive and collaborative decision-making**. My Wife and I joined forces, relying on prayer, strategic planning, and fasting to determine the best course of action for our new home.

During our search, there came a day when we were in the final stages. However, I found myself growing increasingly frustrated to the extent that I expressed my emotions to my wife. I suggested that we should simply lease again, as I was disheartened by the entire process and regretted getting my family in this situation. In response, my wife firmly stated that we absolutely should not do that. She reminded me that we had come too far to turn back and return to the life we were previously leading.

I had a strong desire to reside in Naperville, IL. Unfortunately, we couldn't find any options that met our specific requirements and loan amount. My wife proposed the idea of exploring a different community and beginning anew. Although Naperville was our initial choice, it seemed that fate had other plans for us. Despite my attachment to Naperville, we encountered no favorable circumstances for settling there.

During the entire process, our constant communication with each other and the loan officer resulted in an overwhelming amount of tension, to the point where it felt as if we had become adversaries. We found ourselves engaging in arguments over even the most trivial matters. As I continue to conduct virtual services with my church family while recovering from Covid, the burden of trying to buy a new home has started to take a toll on me.

I made the decision to visit a residence that my wife discovered in Plainfield, IL. The photographs left a lasting impression on me, although my mind couldn't help but dwell on the fact that it wasn't located in Naperville, IL. Upon meeting our real estate agent at the Plainfield property, I couldn't contain my excitement and exclaimed from afar, "That is the house!" A profound sense of certainty resonated within me, and at last, my wife and I were in complete agreement.

The walk through served as a pivotal moment where I truly believed that this long- awaited event was finally becoming a reality. The divine promise of God was on the verge of being fulfilled. Our mutual understanding was crucial in aligning our desires with heaven's will on earth. Often, as husbands, we tend to prioritize our own preferences. However, throughout this journey, God was molding my character and enlightening me about the essence of being a devoted husband and considering my wife as my help meet.

Now it was time to get the clear to close so that we can move our family into this amazing home. This is when things got interesting. The clear to close kept getting rescheduled. Tension has now taken over and my wife and I have a blow out on the day of our Anniversary. August 6, 2021, should have been a day of celebration but it was a day of sword drawing and fierce anger. It seemed as if we were living a nightmare. We became so angry with one another that we decided to drive our separate ways to decide what we would do next. My wife took the girls with her, and I sped off going absolutely nowhere feeling defeated.

During my solitary ride, I prayed, pouring out my heart to God about the unease that had consumed me throughout this entire journey. I pleaded for His peace and comfort, desperately seeking breakthrough. To my surprise, the Lord responded with these profound words. He gently reminded me that His purpose was not to make me comfortable, but to mold my character for the new chapter I had been fervently praying for. Submitted to His voice, my phone buzzed with a text notification. It was my mortgage loan officer, delivering the great news - the clear to close. In that moment, I couldn't contain my joy. It was undoubtedly the most exhilarating text message I had ever received, a testament to the fulfillment of my dreams.

I redirected my car to return and shared the incredible news with my wife. I called her and asked her to meet me back at the hotel parking lot. As we reunited at the parking lot, tears streamed down my face as I revealed the text message I had just received.

Despite the intense argument we had moments ago, she demonstrated her unwavering love for me. "This is the best anniversary gift I could have ever imagined," she whispered softly. My wife is truly the epitome of forgiveness, patience, and love—a remarkable woman any man would be fortunate to have. God knew exactly what I needed.

Here's the back story. Apostle Michelle McClain Walters gave me a prophetic word about the month of

August in 2012. She shared with me that it would be the most incredible month of my life. Naturally, I believed that it would be August of that very year being that I was engaged and anticipating getting married that very month.

Things didn't go that way. Instead of a wedding, the relationship actually came to an end. I had to gather the courage to stand before my church and explain that we were canceling the wedding to remain friends. It was an incredibly embarrassing experience, one that I never could have imagined. Nonetheless, it was a **decision** that had to be made for both of us to be free to marry the person that God had destined for us.

At times, decision-making can become exceedingly difficult when one's emotions are involved and there is a lack of clarity from God. I found myself grappling with the reality that I was pursuing a romantic relationship with a friend, believing that it would thrive due to our long-standing acquaintance. However, God later revealed to me that we were never meant to be anything more than friends. Crossing those boundaries would only bring destruction upon both our lives.

It is crucial to patiently await clarity from God before making decisions driven by emotions, as they will only lead to further shame, harm, and even setbacks. As an unmarried pastor, I was burdened by concerns about what others might think of me. Given my past mistakes in relationships, this posed a significant challenge. Nevertheless, I had to push through the pain.
Hurry up to chapter 3!

Trust in the Lord with all your heart, And lean not on your own understanding; In all your ways acknowledge Him, And He shall [b]direct your paths. Do not be wise in your own eyes; Fear the Lord and depart from evil. It will be health to your [c]flesh, And strength[d] to your bones.
***Proverbs* 3:5-8**
KJV (King James Version)

CHAPTER 3
(Round 3)
PUSH THROUGH THE PAIN

During the years 2013 to 2015, I dedicated myself to obeying the Lord's commands, despite feeling embarrassed about my numerous failed relationships and the frustration of not being able to fully implement the teachings imparted to me by my mother Apostle Karen Hoskins. My mother instilled in us the importance of adhering to the scriptures and conducting our lives in accordance with God's will, with the ultimate goal of pleasing Him. She emphasized that there would be consequences for disregarding God's Word, but also reassured us of His unwavering love. In **Revelation 3:19**, we witness God's love manifested through His merciful chastisement. The greek definition of: **Love** here is *phileó* meaning *(the love of friendship, regard with affection, cherish; I kiss.)* **Rebuke** here is *elegchó* meaning *(to expose, convict, reprove).*

As many as I love, I rebuke and chasten: be zealous therefore, and repent.
Revelation 3:19
KJV (King James Version)

In other words, God's love for you is so immense that He guides you towards the right direction by correcting you. While it may not feel pleasant to be *exposed, convicted, or reproved,* God's love for you is akin to that of a deeply caring friend who is concerned about your future. This realization should motivate you to push through any pain that may arise from your own actions.

In my pursuit of strength and progress in my life, ministry, and future endeavors, I received divine instructions from God to attend a prayer breakfast hosted by someone who had been offended by me. Reluctantly, I complied with this instruction, even though I had no desire to apologize. It perplexed me as to why God would require me to publicly apologize to this individual when I was still healing from my own pain and grievances. Nevertheless, I understood the importance of obeying God's will. Despite the anticipated presence of familiar faces and the curiosity of others regarding my presence, my goal was to please God.

It was during this prayer breakfast that I first laid eyes on my lovely wife, whom I affectionately refer to as **"Pretty Girl"**. She was serving as the armor bearer for the pastor, who happened to be the guest speaker that morning. I attended the event not with the intention of seeking anything or anyone, but rather to purify my conscience and follow the Lord's instructions with hopes of finding healing through my apology.

After Pretty Girl and I started dating, a significant amount of time passed. On **August 6, 2016,** I entered matrimony with the most extraordinary woman on this planet. Then, on **August 20, 2019**, I was blessed with an incredible baby girl named *Ariyah Annice Hester*, who is now 4 years old. Additionally, on **August 6, 2021**, we finalize the purchase of our new home, and on **August**

13, 2021, we were handed the keys and moved into our new home together. It turns out that *Apostle Michelle McClain Walters* was absolutely right. **August** truly turned out to be the most remarkable month of my life that I can vividly recall.

Hence, rather than grappling with one's own ego, adhering to God's commands will ultimately bring forth greater rewards. In Genesis 22, Abraham did not hesitate to follow God's guidance. God commanded him to offer his only son, Isaac, as a sacrifice. The scriptures affirm that Abraham promptly carried out the Lord's instructions.

*And he said, Take now thy son, thine only son Isaac, whom thou lovest, and get thee into the land of Moriah; and **offer him there for a burnt offering** upon one of the mountains which I will tell thee of. And Abraham **rose up early in the morning**, and saddled his ass, and took two of his young men with him, and Isaac his son, and clave the wood for the burnt offering, and rose up, and went unto the place of which God had told him. Then on the third day Abraham lifted up his eyes, and saw the place afar off. And Abraham said unto his young men, Abide ye here with the ass; and I and the lad will go yonder and worship, and come again to you. **And Abraham took the wood of the burnt offering, and laid it upon Isaac his son; and he took the fire in his hand, and a knife; and they went both of them together.***
Genesis 22:2-6
KJV (King James Version)

By obeying God, one is rewarded instead of suffering losses. It leads to victory. Even in times of pain, confusion, or despair, God has a remarkable ability to make the sacrifices worthwhile. Abraham's obedience spared him from sacrificing his son.

And he said, Lay not thine hand upon the lad, neither do thou any thing unto him: for now I know that thou fearest God, seeing thou hast not withheld thy son, thine only son from me. And Abraham lifted up his eyes, and looked, and **behold behind him a ram caught in a thicket by his horns: and Abraham went and took the ram**, *and offered him up for a burnt offering in the stead of his son. And Abraham called the name of that place Jehovahjireh: as it is said to this day, In the mount of the LORD it shall be seen.*
Genesis 22:12-14
KJV (King James Version)

God not only rewards your obedience, but He also blesses you with more than what you were originally willing to sacrifice. Abraham's willingness to sacrifice his only son led him to become the Father of many nations. God wants us to understand the depth of His love for us, which is why He provided His only son as a ram, just as He provided a ram for Abraham. This serves as a powerful motivation to push through your pain, knowing that there is a blessing waiting for us on the other side of our obedience to the Lord.

And the angel of the LORD called unto Abraham out of heaven the second time, And said, By myself have I sworn, saith the LORD, for because thou hast done this thing, and hast not withheld thy son, thine only son: **That in blessing I will bless thee, and in multiplying I will multiply**

thy seed as the stars of the heaven, and as the sand which is upon the sea shore; and thy seed shall possess the gate of his enemies; And in thy seed shall all the nations of the earth be blessed; because thou hast obeyed my voice.
Genesis 22:15-18
KJV (King James Version)

The valuable lesson derived from the testing of your faith is the acquisition of patience, endurance, and the ability to inspire others through your unwavering determination to persevere. According to the book of James, the testing of our faith leads to the development of patience.

Knowing this, that the trying of your faith worketh patience.
James 1:3
KJV (King James Version)

As you persevere through the discomfort, cultivate resilience amidst the trials that challenge your faith. It is crucial to comprehend that God's intention is not to assess your abilities with the expectation of failure. He is an extraordinary Father, aiming to witness your triumph in the test as a result of your diligent efforts and unwavering faith. Pain is an inevitable part of life. As the saying goes, "no pain, no gain." In my opinion, the key to dealing with pain lies in our perspective. Pain often serves as a reflection of life itself. Pain serves as a survival mechanism with the primary objective of safeguarding the body.

In certain instances, persevering through pain can lead to personal growth. Throughout your journey, you will encounter obstacles that demand you to surpass your comfort zone to witness the positive outcomes that lie ahead. It is crucial to make a firm commitment within yourself that giving up is never an option. God has a way of grooming you through your obstacles and making you stronger.

But the God of all grace, who hath called us unto his eternal glory by Christ Jesus, after that ye have suffered a while, make you perfect, stablish, strengthen, settle you.
1 Peter 5:10
KJV (*Kingdom James Version*)

In essence, God's plan is to...
- Restore and renew you.
- Empower you with resilience.
- Render you unyielding and unshakable.
- Establishing you. Making you resolute and concentrated.

Spending time in prayer is crucial for cultivating a proper perspective on the challenges you face. This is particularly important because pain can be bewildering, especially when you believe you don't deserve the suffering you are going through. However, **God has a unique way of utilizing pain to increase your strength as you progress in life.** Your endurance will ultimately become the source of your strength.

Galatians 6:9 emphasizes that we should not grow tired or lose enthusiasm in doing good or living righteously. There is a gratifying outcome for persevering when we lead a righteous life and striving to please God.

And let us not be weary in well doing: for in due season we shall reap, if we faint not.
Galatians 6:9

Christ himself serves as an exceptional exemplar that we can utilize as a blueprint. He, who was faultless, endured a dreadful demise to atone for the world's transgressions and was subsequently bestowed with recompense by His Father for persevering through the agony. Christ now becomes our template and intercessor so that we are not alone while pushing through our agony.

For we have not a high priest which cannot be touched with the feeling of our infirmities; but was in all points tempted like as we are, yet without sin. Let us therefore come boldly unto the throne of grace, that we may obtain mercy, and find grace to help in time of need.
Hebrews 4:15-16

There may come moments when you experience a sense of isolation, believing that nobody comprehends your emotions or concerns, and that nobody can truly empathize with your pain. However, it is important to remember that Jesus Christ understands! He serves as our personal High Priest and source of support. You are not without assistance! You are not solitary! You are not misinterpreted! You are protected and assured through the presence of Christ!

Always keep in mind that God has a divine purpose, a well-crafted plan, and a prophetic promise specifically designed for you, especially during those challenging moments in life. It is crucial to understand that God never intends to burden you with pain or leave you feeling overwhelmed. Instead, He utilizes these difficult times to unveil a new and improved version of yourself. Trust me, I speak from personal experience. I understand the emotions that arise when you question God's timing, eagerly awaiting a breakthrough, pondering over what you may have done wrong, and wondering how He will lead you out of this situation. Rest assured, my friend, that God's ways are beyond our comprehension, and He will guide you towards a brighter future.

Throughout my journey of enduring pain and navigating through challenging times, I have gained a priceless lesson - the unwavering determination to never give up. I have rooted myself in faith, perseverance, and unwavering trust in God. I have never tried any other path, nor have I placed my belief in any other system, for faith is the ultimate driving force in my life. It has this incredible ability to shield me from dwelling on the negative aspects of life. When faced with uncomfortable seasons, faith works wonders by bringing forth a few remarkable transformations:

1. **Faith pleases God:** *But without faith it is **impossible to please him**: for he that cometh to God must believe that he is, and that he is a rewarder of them that diligently seek him.*
   Hebrews 11:6

2. **Faith frames your world:** *Through faith we understand **that the worlds were framed** by the word of God, so that things which are seen were not made of things which do appear.* **Hebrews 11:3**

3. **Faith is a form of obeying God:** *And he that doubteth is damned if he eat, because he eateth not from faith; for **whatsoever is not from faith is sin.** Romans 14:23*

Dealing with pain in life can be an incredibly difficult and personal journey. Here are some valuable strategies that can assist you in navigating through challenging times:

A. **Acknowledge Your Pain:** It is crucial to acknowledge and accept the pain you are experiencing. Ignoring or suppressing it can potentially worsen the situation in the long term. Allow yourself to feel the emotions and understand that it is perfectly alright to not feel okay. This will allow create space to value your victory as you push your way to victory.

B. **Seek Support:** Reach out to someone you trust and confide in them about what you are going through. I would suggest it be one who has experience in the area that you are presently dealing with. Sometimes you may need professional help. Sharing your feelings can help alleviate the burden and provide you with a fresh perspective. There is safety in a multitude of counsel.

C. **Set Small, Achievable Goals:** When faced with adversity, breaking down your challenges into smaller, more manageable tasks can be immensely helpful. This approach allows you to focus on making progress, even if it is one step at a time.

D. **Practice Self Care:** Taking care of yourself is vital during tough times. Ensure that you get enough rest, eat well, exercise, and engage in activities that bring you joy. *DO NOT LOSE YOURSELF!*

E. **Focus On What You Can Control:** Sometimes, certain aspects of painful situations are beyond your control. Instead of dwelling on these, concentrate on the things you can influence. Shifting your focus can help you regain a sense of control. You really must learn how to put all your trust in God.

F. **Discover Your Meaningful Purpose:** Reflect on your values and what gives your life meaning. Engaging in activities that align with your values can help you find and discover your purpose and gain perspective during difficult times.

G. **Learn From Experience:** Although it may be challenging to see in the moment, difficult experiences can provide opportunities for personal growth and learning. Try to find lessons in the pain and use them to become stronger and more resilient.

H. **Be Patient and Kind to Yourself:** Healing and growth takes time. It is okay to experience setbacks, and it is important to be patient and compassionate with yourself as you navigate through the pain. Be very careful not to live cycles.

It is perfectly alright to ask for help when you need it. If you find that the pain in life becomes overwhelming or interferes with your daily life, seeking professional assistance is always essential to experiencing breakthrough.

Don't mistake pushing through the pain for suppressing your emotions or pretending that you're unaffected by the challenges you face. It's about recognizing your feelings, connecting with them, and still finding the determination to overcome until you achieve victory within yourself. Often, we tend to celebrate people's achievements without considering the sacrifices they made to reach their goals. It's important to cultivate a mindset that focuses on winning, regardless of the obstacles, and to celebrate each step of the journey by faith.

You will come to realize that not everyone is obligated to acknowledge your hard work or emotional intelligence, and not everyone will celebrate your successes. But you must find encouragement within yourself and express gratitude to God for guiding you through life's toughest tasks.

Psalm 34:1, David said, "*I will bless the Lord at all times; his praise shall continually be in my mouth.*" He understood the importance of praising God in every situation. Similarly, in **1 Samuel 36:1**, *David encouraged himself in the Lord during a difficult moment in his life.* Despite the distress and criticism, he faced, he
found strength in his faith.

So, let's learn from David's example and push through the pain, acknowledging our feelings but remaining determined to reach victory. God will always see you through when you have to right perspective about life, your circumstances, and your outcome.

CHAPTER
(Round 4)
VALUABLE NIGHTMARES

Once we settled into our brand-new abode, a wave of relief washed over me. "Finally, we can truly unwind and recharge," I whispered to myself. After enduring countless trials and tribulations, I couldn't fathom going through any more challenges. It felt like I had accomplished one of life's greatest dreams. I had married my incredible wife, created a beautiful, blended family, and now we had our dream home.

August 13, 2021, Everything seemed picture-perfect. We were connecting on a whole new level. The joy radiated from my children's faces as they explored their new rooms. They eagerly anticipated the upcoming school year and were excited about growing together as a family. In my mind, nothing could hinder us from celebrating this long- awaited dream come true.

September 21, 2022, Unfortunately, my vision started to blur, my thirst became unquenchable, and I found myself making frequent trips to the bathroom. I was completely clueless about what was happening to me. Seeking guidance, I confided in my wife and expressed my urgency to visit the emergency room to discover the cause of my symptoms.

Upon reaching the emergency room and receiving attention from the nurse, I was diagnosed with type 2 diabetes, with my glucose level measuring at a staggering 457. The news hit me like a ton of bricks. I felt devastated. Being unaware of the intricacies of type 2 diabetes, my mind immediately conjured up the worst-case scenarios. My once cherished dream had transformed into a dreadful nightmare.

I was completely shattered, shedding tears for weeks as I felt utterly defeated. The stress and fear had taken such a toll on me that my blood pressure skyrocketed to 166/111. I found myself rushing to the emergency room multiple times, desperately seeking solace. Thankfully, one of the doctors not only enlightened me but also empowered me to conquer my fears. With his guidance, I embraced a new lifestyle - altering my diet, engaging in regular exercise, and striving to maintain a stress-free existence. With the power of prayer and unwavering support from my family, I embarked on a journey to reverse the type 2 diabetes that had been diagnosed. Every single day, I dedicated myself to exercise, tirelessly walking on my treadmill. Over the course of six months, I shredded off 74 pounds, going from 353 pounds to 279 pounds. What was once a vicious nightmare had now become a valuable nightmare.

These are the experiences that may seem devastating, but God has a specific purpose and plan for allowing them to occur in your life. Although we may perceive them as nightmares, they hold great value. Years ago, God had already directed me to prioritize my health. As an itinerant minister of the gospel, it is crucial for me to take care of my well-being to withstand travels, intense services, and the responsibility of serving God's people at such a profound level.

It is of utmost significance that we alter our perspectives to acknowledge the presence of God in our lives amidst various challenges. Failing to appreciate the obstacles we encounter can cause us to overlook moments of triumph, which are often born out of these very obstacles. Here are five principles that can aid in cultivating such a mindset:

1. **Express Gratitude:** Regularly take the time to acknowledge and appreciate the positive aspects of your life, even when faced with challenges. Keeping a gratitude journal, where you jot down things you are thankful for, can be a beneficial practice.

2. **Focus on Solutions:** Instead of dwelling on problems, train yourself to concentrate on potential solutions. When confronted with a challenge, ask yourself, "What can I do to improve this situation?" Shifting your focus from the problem to the solution can help you maintain a positive perspective.

3. **Embrace Change:** Understand that change is a natural part of life, and although it may bring challenges, it also presents new opportunities. Embracing change with an open and adaptable mindset can assist you in navigating challenges more effectively and maintaining a positive attitude.

4. **Foster Self-Compassion:** Treat yourself with kindness and understanding, particularly during difficult times. Recognize that everyone faces challenges, and it is acceptable to not be perfect. Practicing self-compassion can help you maintain a

positive mindset and recover from setbacks.

5. **Surround Yourself with Positivity:** Surround yourself with supportive and positive individuals who uplift and encourage you. Engage in activities that bring you joy and fulfillment, and limit exposure to negative influences that can dampen your mindset.

By embracing these principles, you can develop a more determined and positive mindset, enabling you to navigate life's challenges with grace and optimism.

Recognizing the worth of valuable nightmares is a difficult endeavor, and they are not always acknowledged as such. At times, these unsettling encounters endure longer than desired, making it difficult to grasp their significance. A change in perspective and the possession of patience are undoubtedly necessary to truly comprehend their value. Certain individuals in the Word of God come to mind when I think of valuable nightmares or having to utilize patience.

- **Abraham** displayed great patience as he awaited the fulfillment of God's promise. Eventually, he received what was promised to him. Despite Sarah's advanced age, they were blessed with a son, Isaac, after a long period of waiting. The Lord remained faithful to His word and fulfilled His promise to Sarah, just as He had said.

(Genesis 21:1-5)

- **Joseph** endured mistreatment from his own brothers, being sold into slavery, and encountered numerous challenges, Joseph's unwavering faithfulness to the Lord is truly remarkable. He remained faithful and true to God through it all. (*Genesis 45:4-8*)

- **David** endured continuous harassment from King Saul and was frequently forced to flee to evade Saul's relentless pursuit to end his life. However, David consistently refrained from taking matters into his own hands. Despite having the chance to eliminate Saul, he chose not to. Instead, he patiently awaited God's divine judgment and trusted that everything would unfold according to God's perfect timing. (*1 Samuel 24:8-13*)

According to God's Word, we are encouraged to find joy in every temptation we face, as we understand that it strengthens our faith and cultivates patience within us. You are being built, developed, changed, strengthened, and sometimes restored. It is in the midst of valuable nightmares that you're being completed and fulfilled.

*My brethren, count it all joy when ye fall into divers temptations; Knowing this, that the trying of your faith worketh patience. But **let patience have her perfect work, that ye may be perfect and entire**, wanting nothing.*
James 1:2-4, KJV (*King James Version*)

Patience and perspective are the key when dealing with tough seasons in life. Most individuals find it difficult to believe that a nightmare can hold any value. Yet again, one's perspective plays a crucial role. There are certain events in life that are necessary for personal growth, maturity, and the development of a better version of oneself. If we consider the sport of boxing, it is common for most boxers to begin their journey as amateurs. They build their records, acquire their skillset, and gradually gain popularity from their humble beginnings.

I vividly recall the 1996 Summer Olympics, where a Bulgarian boxer named Serafim Todorov and Floyd Mayweather Jr. competed in a three-round boxing match, with Mayweather representing the USA. Many believed that Mayweather had outperformed the Bulgarian boxer. However, to everyone's surprise, when the fight concluded, the referee raised Mayweather's hand, but the announcer and scorekeepers declared Todorov as the winner. It left everyone stunned. Mayweather, in his post-fight interview, expressed his disappointment and shed tears, as this experience must have felt like a nightmare for him.

Nevertheless, this seemingly devastating setback turned out to be an incredibly valuable lesson for Mayweather. It motivated him to pursue a professional boxing career. As a result, he currently holds an impressive boxing record of 50-0, with 27 knockouts and 12 world championships across five weight classes. Mayweather's professional journey exemplifies the significance of valuable nightmares. Even if you have encountered something terrible in your own life, it is important to remember that you are still a winner, regardless of how others perceive your situation. These experiences have the potential to shape the champion within you.

Throughout my personal journey, I have encountered numerous challenges that required me to persevere to transition from one phase of life to another. For 11 years of my 18-year tenure as a Pastor, I remained unmarried, which presented its own set of difficulties. I faced failed relationships, struggled with poor credit, witnessed individuals departing from the church for various reasons, and encountered disappointment within my ministry. While some of these obstacles could have been avoided, there were certain circumstances that were simply unavoidable. However, it was through these experiences that I was able to cultivate personal growth, maturity, and ultimately develop into the leader I am today.

Valuing nightmares can be a complex and personal matter, but there are several key core values to consider when approaching this topic:

1. **Self-Reflection:** Recognizing the significance of nightmares and utilizing them as a tool for self-reflection and personal development.

2. **Emotional Insight:** Appreciating the value of nightmares in gaining insight into one's emotions and addressing unresolved issues or fears.

3. **Psychological Exploration:** Regarding nightmares as a glimpse into the subconscious mind and an opportunity for psychological exploration and understanding.

4. **Building Inner Strength:** Recognizing nightmares

to build resilience and develop coping strategies, ultimately fostering mental strength and well-being.

5. **Symbolic Interpretation:** Embracing the symbolic nature of nightmares and acknowledging their potential to convey important messages or warnings.

6. **Healing and Transformation:** Viewing nightmares as a catalyst for healing and transformation, motivating individuals to confront their fears and work through past traumas.

Like Mayweather, there have been moments where I should have emerged as the winner, only to be let down by loss, abandonment, and betrayal. However, I have fully embraced these core values as my own personal coping mechanism during some of the most difficult times in my life. I am grateful to God for walking me through my personal struggles and leading me to victory. By embracing these core values, individuals can approach nightmares in life with purpose and understanding, leading to personal growth and overall well-being.

Previously, I shared my ordeal of living in a hotel for four months, being diagnosed with type 2 diabetes, and ultimately overcoming the diagnosis through dietary changes and regular exercise and entered a remarkable phase in our lives still excited about our future.

We were involved in a Network Marketing Company where my wife and I achieved tremendous success by assisting clients with our services and building a substantial team of 13 thousand individuals over time.

We mentored individuals who earned six- figure incomes and amassed a significant amount of wealth ourselves. My wife became a six-figure earner, while I reached the seven-figure mark within the company. I had officially become a documented millionaire, fulfilling yet another dream. Witnessing so many people achieve financial stability and security was truly remarkable.

Unfortunately, our company was ultimately forced to shut down due to actions taken by the FTC (*Federal Trade Commission*). Once again, we found ourselves confronted with a daunting and distressing situation. However, we remained steadfast in our faith. We received instructions to maintain the unity of our teams and continue working on a different platform while our organization resolved the ongoing issues with the FTC. However, contrary to expectations, the situation turned out to be disastrous as the teams failed to stay together.

To prioritize the preservation of relationships, which held utmost importance to me, I decided to part ways with a group that I had previously mentored. I prioritized morals over money, valuing family over fame and loyalty over luxury. After the company reopened, we ended up moving on without any compensation. It is possible to go from being a millionaire today to relying on government assistance tomorrow. This highlights the crucial significance of maintaining humility.

Throughout these encounters, you will encounter fear, anxiety, frustration, anger, depression, and occasionally even unforgiveness. It is crucial to maintain a pure heart, as when you place your trust in God during challenging times, He may be evaluating your response to the situation. Responding inappropriately can have severe consequences, while responding with righteousness can elevate you to a better state than before. Always bear in mind that it all boils down to perspective. God wants you to understand that He remains unchanged in the darkness, just as He does when your circumstances are favorable and full of light.

Walking by faith during tough times can be challenging, but it's a central aspect of the life of a believer. Here are some ways to walk by faith when things are rough, along with scriptural references from Word of God:

- **Prayer**: Turn to prayer as a source of strength and guidance. **Philippians 4:6-7** says, "Do not be anxious about anything, but in everything by prayer and supplication with thanksgiving let your requests be made known to God. And the peace of God, which surpasses all understanding, will guard your hearts and your minds in Christ Jesus."

- **Seeking God's Word**: Spend time studying the Word of God to find comfort and wisdom. **Romans 10:17** states, "So faith comes from hearing, and hearing through the word of Christ."

- **Trusting in God's Plan**: Trust that God has a plan, even when things seem difficult. **Proverbs 3:5-6** advises, "Trust in the Lord with all your heart, and do not lean on your own understanding. In all your ways acknowledge him, and he will make straight your paths."

- **Community Support**: Lean on your faith community for support and encouragement. **Hebrews 10:24-25** says, "And let us consider how to stir up one another to love and good works, not neglecting to meet together, as is the habit of some, but encouraging one another, and all the more as you see the Day drawing near."

- **Gratitude**: Practice gratitude and thankfulness, even in the midst of challenges. **1 Thessalonians 5:16-18** advises, "Rejoice always, pray without ceasing, give thanks in all circumstances; for this is the will of God in Christ Jesus for you."

- **Perseverance**: Endure through faith, knowing that trials can produce perseverance and character. **James 1:2-4** encourages, "Count it all joy, my brothers, when you meet trials of various kinds, for you know that the testing of your faith produces steadfastness. And let steadfastness have its full effect, that you may be perfect and complete, lacking in nothing.

By incorporating these practices into your life and focusing on the promises and teachings of the Word of God, you can walk by faith during rough times. The believer is expected to walk by faith, and not by sight. Turn your nightmares into lessons for the future and view life through the lenses of God. Things are changing for you right now, as you read this book.

You should express gratitude towards God for the obstacles that you encounter, as they possess the potential to mold you into God's idea of you. These challenges serve as valuable lessons for future generations. Remember, the majority of what you experience is not solely about you or your current circumstances. It plays a significant role in establishing a blueprint for the future. Moreover, any weapons that may be formed against you will not succeed, as stated in **Isaiah 54:17**. Rest assured, God will ensure your vindication.

No weapon that is formed against thee shall prosper; and every tongue that shall rise against thee in judgment thou shalt condemn. This is the heritage of the servants of the LORD, and their righteousness is of me, saith the LORD.
Isaiah 54:17
KJV *(King James Version)*

CHAPTER
(Round 5)
BIRTHING AFTER THE BREAKING

A pregnancy is commonly divided into three trimesters, with each trimester spanning around three months. There are instances when life mirrors a pregnancy, encompassing a process that is necessary for new beginnings to emerge. Here is a brief overview of each trimester:

First Trimester (Week 1 to Week 12):
- This is the earliest stage of pregnancy.
- The fertilized egg implants in the uterus, and the embryo begins to develop.
- Major organs and body systems start to form.
- Many women experience symptoms such as morning sickness, fatigue, and breast tenderness during this time.

Second Trimester (Week 13 to Week 26):
- This is often considered the most enjoyable trimester for many women.
- The baby's movements can usually be felt by the mother.
- The baby's sex can often be determined through ultrasound during this trimester.
- Many of the early pregnancy symptoms, such as nausea and fatigue, start to decrease.

Third Trimester (Week 27 to Birth):
- The baby continues to grow and develop rapidly.

- The mother's abdomen grows significantly, and she may experience discomfort due to the baby's size and position.
- Braxton Hicks contractions, which are practice contractions, may occur.
- As the due date approaches, the mother may experience more frequent medical checkups to monitor the baby's growth and position.

It's important to note that every pregnancy is unique, and the experience of each trimester can vary from woman to woman. Ultimately, having a midwife or a support system is essential for the success of the birth.

This same overview has so many similarities to real life experiences and seasons. Let us look at things from a spiritual point of view using the same information above as a template for birthing spiritually.

First Trimester (0 - 3rd Month):
- This is the earliest stage of discovering your purpose and or calling.
- The time you spend with God and being discipled causes you to grow and develop.
- Your disciplined time spent with the Lord produces clarity concerning your purpose.
- Many individuals experience certain levels of spiritual warfare during this time.

Second Trimester (3rd - 6th Month):
- This is often considered the identity stage; you are now showing signs of maturity.
- Your leader or mentor now acknowledges what God has called you to do.

- Things become clearer and you become more experienced with spiritual warfare.

Third Trimester (6th - 9th Month):
- You are growing more rapidly and coming into your full purpose and identity.
- You begin experiencing different levels of discomfort and spiritual warfare.
- This is the level that you are truly paying a price for the grace on your life.
- At this point you are spending more personal with your leader to be develop.

Spiritual warfare at this point is embraced as your apostolic career and you are aware of the responsibility of protecting the grace that is in your life. Challenges, obstacles, and circumstances can be likened to intense contractions. The proximity of these contractions in terms of time indicates the urgency to prepare for the final push, leading to the birth of new possibilities.

It is crucial to approach life and your purpose with a similar perspective. As you strive towards fulfilling your life's purpose and striving to become a better version of yourself, it is important to perceive the ongoing challenges as indicators of your proximity to a breakthrough. Although it may be painful, these challenges are aiding in your personal growth. Despite the discomfort, you are maturing through these experiences. Even though things may be happening rapidly, remember that you are on the verge of embracing the newness that God has promised. Therefore, be prepared to persevere through it all and step into your new chapter and get ready to push.

During the process of childbirth, it is customary to have the assistance of midwives to facilitate the delivery of the newborn baby. Similarly, in the realm of spirituality, it is crucial to have seasoned individuals in your life who can mentor and support you through life's trials, helping you navigate through difficult times until you achieve your desired transformation. Spend time praying for the right people. It is extremely important to not allow the wrong individuals in your space or life during this critical time of transformation.

Everyone possesses a unique purpose, talents, gifts, and even callings. It is expected of you by God to exert efforts to learn and uncover all these aspects about yourself. In addition, there are numerous individuals who have already acquired the knowledge and skills necessary for you to fulfill your assignment. It is crucial that you connect with these individuals.

From a spiritual perspective, our journey through life can often be compared to the process of pregnancy. Just as some women carry the potential for new life, others carry the promises of what is to come, and some carry the greatness within them. I firmly believe that we all go through seasons that resemble the act of giving birth.

The very thing that you have been carrying, whether it be a gift, talent, responsibility, or even a heartfelt request, will soon manifest itself as a reality. It is crucial that you do not give up or quit during the challenging and painful moments that resemble contractions. Remember, the frequency and intensity of contractions during labor determine how soon a woman can push her newborn baby into the world. This principle applies to life as well. The greater the challenges you face, the more difficult the task may seem, and the stronger the attacks on your life become, it is often a sign that you are on the verge of stepping into the very thing you have been praying for.

During the waiting process can frequently give rise to feelings of anxiety and sometimes even depression. It is crucial to cultivate a deep trust in God during this phase of your life. Remember that the same God who permits you to experience challenges is also the one who possesses the power to guide you through them. Placing your trust in Him is of utmost significance. Your inner tranquility will be discovered in God until the moment of your deliverance or breakthrough arrives.

The Word of God encourages us in understanding the correct way to exercise patience while waiting for God. Especially when it seems as if He is not ready to assist you towards birthing your purposes.

*Be still before the Lord and **wait patiently for him; fret not yourself** over the one who prospers in his way, over the man who carries out evil devices!*
Psalm 37:7
ESV *(English Standard Version)*

So the LORD must wait for you to come to him so he can show you his love and compassion. For the LORD is a faithful God. Blessed are those who wait for his help.
Isaiah 30:18
NLT *(New Living Translation)*

Waiting on God for deliverance requires patience, trust, and reliance on His timing and wisdom. Here are seven principles along with corresponding scriptural references:

Trust in God's Timing:
- *Scripture:* **Psalm 27:14 (NIV)** - "Wait for the Lord; be strong and take heart and wait for the Lord."

Seek God's Guidance:
- *Scripture:* **Proverbs 3:5-6 (NIV)** - "Trust in the Lord with all your heart and lean not on your own understanding; in all your ways submit to him, and he will make your paths straight."

Persistent Prayer:
- *Scripture:* **Philippians 4:6-7 (NIV)** - "Do not be anxious about anything, but in every situation, by prayer and petition, with thanksgiving, present your requests to God. And the peace of God, which transcends all understanding, will guard your hearts and your minds in Christ Jesus."

Maintain Faith and Hope:
- *Scripture:* **Hebrews 11:1 (NIV)** - "Now faith is confidence in what we hope for and assurance about what we do not see."

God's Promises are Sure:
- *Scripture:* **2 Peter 1:4 (NIV)** - "Through these he has given us his very great and precious promises, so that through them you may participate in the divine nature, having escaped the corruption in the world caused by evil desires."

Wait with Patience:
- *Scripture:* **Psalm 37:7 (NIV)** - "Be still before the Lord and wait patiently for him; do not fret when people succeed in their ways, when they carry out their wicked schemes."

Rest in God's Sovereignty:
- *Scripture:* **Romans 8:28 (NIV) - "And we know that in all things God works for the good of those who love him, who have been called according to his purpose."**

Therefore, waiting on God is an active process of trusting and seeking Him, not a passive resignation. These principles can serve as a foundation for a strong and enduring faith as you wait on God for deliverance.

Having the right mindset is crucial when attempting to birth your purpose. A focused mindset can significantly impact your ability to discover, pursue, and fulfill your life's purpose. Here are eight significant assets for cultivating the appropriate mindset:

1. **Clarity and Vision:** A positive mindset helps provide clarity about your purpose and allows you to envision your goals more clearly. When you have a clear vision, you can better align your actions and decisions with your overarching life purpose.

2. **Perseverance:** Pursuing your purpose often involves facing challenges and setbacks. A positive mindset enhances your resilience and perseverance, enabling you to overcome obstacles with

determination and optimism.

3. **Openness to Learning:** Having the right mindset involves being open to new ideas, experiences, and continuous learning. This openness allows you to adapt to changing circumstances, refine your purpose, and grow personally and professionally.

4. **Courage to Take Risks:** Achieving your purpose may require stepping out of your comfort zone and taking calculated risks. A positive mindset fosters courage, empowering you to embrace challenges and take the necessary steps toward fulfilling your purpose.

5. **Increased Motivation:** A positive mindset is often associated with increased motivation and enthusiasm. When you are motivated, you are more likely to stay committed to your goals and put in the necessary effort to bring your purpose to fruition.

6. **Healthy Self-Image:** Believing in yourself and having a healthy self-image are essential components of the right mindset. When you value your capabilities and potential, you are more likely to pursue your purpose with confidence and conviction.

7. **Responsible Decision-Making:** The right mindset encourages responsible decision-making. You become more intentional about the choices you make, ensuring that they align with your purpose and contribute positively to your journey.

8. **Optimism and Positivity:** Maintaining a positive outlook fosters optimism and positivity. It allows you to approach challenges with a hopeful mindset, finding solutions and opportunities even in difficult situations.

I want to place emphasizes on the importance of staying focused on birthing purpose despite the challenges and anxieties that life may bring. Here are some additional thoughts to reinforce this message:

- **Guard Your Focus:** Be intentional about where you direct your attention. While challenges and anxieties are inevitable, make a conscious effort to focus on your purpose and the steps you can take to move closer to it. Avoid being consumed by negative distractions.

- **Lean on Support Systems:** Surround yourself with a supportive network of friends, family, mentors, or like-minded individuals who understand your journey and can provide encouragement during difficult times. Sharing your burdens makes them more bearable.

- **Practice Self-Care:** As I stated earlier, take care of your physical, mental, and emotional well-being. Regular self-care activities, such as exercise, mindfulness, and adequate rest, can help you manage stress and anxiety, allowing you to stay focused on your purpose.

- **Set Realistic Expectations:** Acknowledge that challenges are part of the journey, and setbacks don't define your worth or potential. Set realistic expectations for yourself and recognize that progress often involves overcoming obstacles.

- **Learn to Adapt:** Life is dynamic, and circumstances may change. Be adaptable and willing to adjust your plans or strategies when necessary. Flexibility is a key component of navigating the uncertainties of life without compromising your purpose.

- **Celebrate Small Wins:** Acknowledge and celebrate the small victories along the way. Recognizing your progress, no matter how incremental, can boost your confidence and motivation, helping you stay on course.

- **Remain Grounded in Your Values:** Your values are the foundation of your purpose. When faced with challenges, refer to your core values to guide your decisions and actions. This can provide stability and clarity during turbulent times.

By maintaining focus, resilience, and a positive mindset, you can navigate challenges without allowing them to derail your progress or cause you to miscarry your purpose in life. God will help you carry things out all the way. Be patient and give birth!

Be encouraged and know that God will never allow you to miscarry your purpose if you stick to His plan and follow, is instructions. It is also important to note having spiritual midwives in your life can be profoundly important when birthing your purpose, particularly if your purpose is deeply rooted in your spiritual beliefs or if you seek spiritual guidance along your journey. Here are some reasons why spiritual midwives can play a crucial role in the process:

- **Spiritual Insight:** Spiritual midwives can provide valuable spiritual insights and perspectives that align with your beliefs. They can help you discern the spiritual aspects of your purpose and guide you in understanding how your purpose connects to your spiritual journey.

- **Prayer and Intercession:** Spiritual midwives are often individuals who are committed to prayer and intercession. They can pray with you and for you, seeking divine guidance, protection, and favor as you pursue your purpose.

- **Alignment with Values:** If your purpose is closely tied to your spiritual values, having spiritual midwives ensures that the guidance you receive aligns with those values. They can help you stay true to your beliefs and navigate ethical and moral dilemmas.

- **Scriptural Wisdom:** Spiritual midwives may draw upon scriptural wisdom to provide guidance. They can help you find relevant passages or teachings that offer inspiration and direction for your purpose journey.

- **Encouragement through Faith:** During challenging times, spiritual midwives can provide encouragement grounded in faith. They may remind you of biblical stories of perseverance, faith, and triumph to inspire and strengthen your resolve.

- **Prophetic Assistance with Time:** Spiritual midwives may assist you in discerning the divine timing of your purpose. Understanding God's timing can be crucial, as it aligns your journey with a higher plan and helps you remain patient and trusting.

- **Spiritual Accountability:** Spiritual midwives can act as accountability partners in your spiritual walk. They may help you stay committed to your values and spiritual practices, ensuring that your pursuit of purpose is grounded in a strong spiritual foundation.

- **Facilitation of Spiritual Growth:** The journey of birthing your purpose is not only about fulfilling external goals but also about spiritual growth. Spiritual midwives can coach you in this process, helping you deepen your relationship with your faith and spiritual practices.

- **Creation of a Sacred Space:** Having spiritual midwives creates a sacred and supportive space for you to explore and express your spiritual connection to your purpose. This nurturing environment can foster a deeper sense of purpose and meaning.

- **Integration of Faith and Purpose:** Spiritual midwives help integrate your faith and purpose, showing you how your spiritual beliefs are interconnected with your life's calling. This integration brings a holistic perspective to your purpose journey.

While not everyone may have spiritual beliefs, for those who do, having spiritual midwives can provide a unique and essential layer of support, guidance, and encouragement as you navigate the path of birthing your purpose in alignment with your spiritual convictions.

In the Word of God, there are several individuals who played significant roles in guiding and supporting others in their spiritual journeys. Here are three major spiritual midwives from the Bible:

Moses: Moses served as a spiritual midwife for the Israelites, leading them out of slavery in Egypt and guiding them toward the Promised Land. His role was not only political and military but deeply spiritual. He communicated with God, received the commandments on Mount Sinai, and provided spiritual leadership to a nation. Moses' guidance and intercession on behalf of the Israelites exemplify the role of a spiritual midwife in leading a community toward its divine purpose.

Elijah: Elijah was a prophet in the Old Testament who played a crucial spiritual midwifery role for his successor, Elisha. Elijah mentored Elisha, guiding him in the ways of the Lord and passing on the prophetic mantle. Elijah's role demonstrates the importance of mentorship and spiritual guidance in the development and continuation of a prophetic calling.

Elizabeth (Mother of John the Baptist): Elizabeth, the mother of John the Baptist, played a spiritual midwife role in recognizing and supporting Mary, the mother of

Jesus. When Mary visited Elizabeth during her pregnancy, Elizabeth, filled with the Holy Spirit, recognized the significance of Mary's child. Elizabeth's affirmation and blessing contributed to Mary's spiritual strength and resolve as she carried out her unique purpose in giving birth to Jesus.

Apostle Paul would fit the description as well. While the term "*midwife*" is not used to describe Apostle Paul in the Bible, there are several aspects of his ministry that align with the concept of spiritual guidance, mentorship, and nurturing, which are akin to the role of a midwife in the spiritual sense. Here are some signs from Paul's writings and actions:

- **Mentorship and Discipleship:** Paul engaged in intentional mentorship and discipleship with individuals like Timothy. In **2 Timothy 2:2 (NIV)**, Paul instructs Timothy: "And the things you have heard me say in the presence of many witnesses entrust reliable people who will also be qualified to teach others." This reflects a generational and mentorship approach to passing on spiritual teachings.

- **Spiritual Fatherhood:** Paul referred to himself as a spiritual father to those he ministered to. In **1 Corinthians 4:15 (NIV)**, he states, "Even if you had ten thousand guardians in Christ, you do not have many fathers, for in Christ Jesus I became your father through the gospel." This language emphasizes a sense of spiritual parenthood and responsibility.

- **Laboring in Prayer:** Paul's letters often express his deep concern and labor in prayer for the spiritual well-being of the communities he ministered to. In **Colossians 1:28-29 (NIV),** he writes: "We proclaim him, admonishing and teaching everyone with all wisdom, so that we may present everyone fully mature in Christ. To this end, I strenuously contend with all the energy Christ so powerfully works in me." This indicates his earnest desire for the spiritual maturity of believers.

- **Providing Spiritual Guidance:** Paul's letters are filled with practical advice and spiritual guidance for the communities he wrote to. For example, in **Ephesians 4:11-13** (NIV), he speaks about the roles of apostles, prophets, evangelists, pastors, and teachers in equipping and building up the body of Christ for maturity.

- **Encouragement in Challenges:** Paul often encouraged and exhorted believers facing challenges. In **2 Corinthians 1:3-4 (NIV)**, he expresses this role of comfort: "Praise be to the God and Father of our Lord Jesus Christ, the Father of compassion and the God of all comfort, who comforts us in all our troubles so that we can comfort those in any trouble with the comfort we ourselves receive from God."

While the term "midwife" may not be explicitly used, these aspects of Paul's ministry reflect a deep commitment to the spiritual growth, development, and well-being of the early Christian communities—a role like that of a spiritual midwife.

These biblical figures showcase the importance of spiritual guidance, mentorship, and support in the context of fulfilling one's divine purpose. They not only provided physical leadership but also served as conduits for God's guidance and spiritual insight. Their stories serve as inspiration for individuals seeking spiritual midwives in their own lives as they navigate their purpose and relationship with God.

Who are the spiritual midwives in your life and what role have you given them in your journey to birthing your purpose in life?

_____

_____

_____

_____

_____

_____

_____

Ultimately, these are individuals who assist you in navigating through the difficult moments in life that ultimately lead to success, rewards, and sometimes even new beginnings. Regardless of the circumstances, it is crucial not to give up. Throughout the process of writing this book, I encountered numerous challenges.

However, I made a conscious decision not to succumb to the negative influences. Instead, I chose to adopt a perspective aligned with God's Word.

I persevered through a period of chronic anxiety and depression. There were mornings when I woke up feeling overwhelmed by despair and defeat. Some days, I felt disconnected from my own family. Depression consumed me with thoughts of past failures and losses, while anxiety plagued me with worries about the future and the worst possible outcomes.

Fortunately, I had a support system of people who helped me navigate through these difficult times. I am immensely grateful to God for my Wife, who stood by my side unwaveringly, even during moments when I couldn't control my tears. As you read this book, I hope you remember, just as I did, that God inhabits the praises of His people. He desires to exchange your burdens for a sense of joy and gratitude. All you need to do is commit to praising Him, even when you don't fully comprehend the situation.

> *I will bless the LORD at all times: his praise shall continually be in my mouth.*
> **Psalm 34:1 KJV (*King James Version*)**

Just like a woman whose water bag breaks and goes through the birthing stage, there is nothing quite like the moment when her healthy newborn baby is placed in her arms after all the turmoil. She may be tired, in pain, and not feeling as attractive, but she is filled with relief and overwhelming joy. Remember, no matter what, you must go through the process of birthing after the breaking.

There is something that God has placed on the inside of us all that can change the lives of others, but we first must push it forth. God has given you the blueprint in His Word and we must depend on Him to bring things to full manifestation and not abort our purposes in life. There will be days of stress, anxiety, depression and even fear which all fall under the spirit of heaviness. However, you must remember **Isaiah 61:3** and declare it over your life!

To appoint unto them that mourn in Zion, to give unto them beauty for ashes, the oil of joy for mourning, the garment of praise for the spirit of heaviness; that they might be called trees of righteousness, the planting of the LORD, that he might be glorified.
Isaiah 61:3 KJV (King James Version)

The antidote to heaviness is praise! You must praise your way through and give birth to the very thing that you're carrying for an entirely new generation of people. There is something within you that is meant for someone else. Keep pushing, persevering, and even if necessary, vocalizing your frustrations, but never give up on your purpose!

I'm writing this book right now, dealing with an extreme amount of anxiety and mental stress but God is bringing me through, and I am already victorious! I thank God for the support system that he's given me and my ability to change my perspective and see God in what has seemed to be one of the worst seasons of life for me. I bless the Lord for it all now because I get to walk away a champion and able to pour into you as you.

CHAPTER
(Round 6)
PUTTING THINGS INTO PERSPECTIVE

Perspective has multiple meanings depending on the context in which it is used. Here are a few common definitions:

- **Point of View or Attitude:** Perspective can also refer to a person's point of view or attitude towards a particular subject, issue, or situation. It involves the way someone perceives and interprets information based on their personal experiences, beliefs, and values.

- **Spatial Relations or Position:** In a general sense, perspective can refer to the spatial relationship between objects or the way things are positioned in relation to each other. For example, looking at a situation from a different perspective might mean considering it from a different angle or viewpoint.

- **Context or Frame of Reference:** Perspective can be synonymous with context or frame of reference. It's about how a situation, problem, or idea is viewed within a certain context, which can influence one's understanding or interpretation.

- **Philosophical Perspective:** In philosophy, perspective can be related to a particular philosophical standpoint or worldview. Different philosophical perspectives offer unique interpretations of reality, knowledge, and existence.

Understanding the specific context in which the term *"perspective"* is used is crucial to interpreting its meaning accurately. Hence, in this Chapter, our specific aim is to concentrate on gaining a **contextual or referential frame of reference** when putting things into perspective.

After encountering numerous difficult seasons in life, I have acquired the wisdom to view things from a balanced standpoint. Life revolves around acquiring knowledge, improving oneself, and achieving success, all of which allow God to shine through our lives to impact others. By continuing in a state of bitterness, unforgiveness, and brokenness, you jeopardize the opportunity to learn vital lessons that will be indispensable in the forthcoming seasons and days to come.

Different people and different stages of your life rely on you to have a clear and accurate understanding of things to execute at the next level. Remember, your seasons in life are prophetic and must be lived according to a certain template.
Part of that template is being sure that your mindset concerning the negative things in your life does not interfere with your future judgements and decision making. The lack of healing of the past can affect your decisions in the future.

Maintaining a positive perspective in the face of negative experiences can be challenging, but it is a valuable skill for personal growth and well-being. Here are three ways to cultivate a positive outlook:

Find the Silver Lining:
- *Look for lessons:* Consider what you can learn from the negative experience. Every challenge offers an opportunity for personal growth and development. Reflect on the lessons you can take away from the situation.
- *Appreciate the contrast:* Negative experiences can help you appreciate the positive aspects of life even more. Use them as a contrast to highlight the things you might have taken for granted and develop a deeper sense of gratitude.

Practice Mindfulness and Acceptance:
- *Be present in the moment:* Instead of dwelling on past negative experiences or worrying about the future, focus on the present. Mindfulness techniques, such as meditation and deep breathing, can help you stay grounded and reduce anxiety. *This stage holds immense significance in shaping your future.*
- *Acceptance of what you cannot change:* Acknowledge that some events are beyond your control. By accepting the reality of a situation, you can redirect your energy toward things you can influence and change. This attitude shift can foster a positive mindset.

Reframe Negative Thoughts:
- *Challenge negative beliefs:* Examine your thoughts and challenge any negative or irrational beliefs you may hold about the situation. Ask yourself if there are alternative perspectives or interpretations that might be more positive.

- *Reframe with positivity:* Instead of viewing a negative experience as a failure, see it as an opportunity for growth. Focus on what you gained from the experience or how it might contribute to your resilience. Reframing negative thoughts can transform your outlook.

It is so unfortunate that some individuals lack the ability to find the silver lining in difficult situations. Consequently, they are unable to envision a brighter future or find closure regarding the challenging experiences that have shaped them, despite the discomfort. Gaining this skill has allowed me to see why all the things labeled negative in my life had to take place. By sharing my triumphs during each season, I have positively influenced numerous others. The key to seeing through the darkness lies in maintaining a proper perspective.

Being born with a disease and enduring pain crisis most of my youth was the prerequisite of me being able to minister healing and deliverance to others as a servant of God. I have since witnessed countless individuals receive miracles after attending a service at our church or during an itinerant assignment in ministry.

The failed relationships I have experienced truly prepared me for my marriage, of which I have used all my lessons from the past to develop a strong lasting marriage with my amazing wife. In addition, the mistakes I have made as a pastor became the lessons, I have used to relaunch Gods church with the heart to endure without any regrets.

Living with regret will often dismiss the lessons you have learned and will only highlight the negative experiences instead. Both are important but it is more important to come out of your experiences with victory on your mind and lessons to leverage.

Hard times reward you with an advantage. You learn how to see victory in the midst of a difficult or unpleasant situation. Faith is the sole means to exist in a realm of understanding and perception. To enhance your faith, it is essential to delve deep within yourself and acknowledge that God has a specific intention behind the challenges you face in life. Find encouragement in scriptures like the ones below:

Don't be afraid, for I am with you. Don't be discouraged, for I am your God. I will strengthen you and help you. I will hold you up with my victorious right hand.
Isaiah 41:10

"I have told you all this so that you may have peace in me. Here on earth you will have many trials and sorrows. But take heart, because I have overcome the world."
John 16:33

Don't worry about anything; instead, pray about everything. Tell God what you need, and thank him for all he has done. Then you will experience God's peace, which exceeds anything we can understand. His peace will guard your hearts and minds as you live in Christ Jesus.
Philippians 4:6-7

More than ever before, we must be attentive to God's instructions. It is crucial for us to grasp onto the Word of God and steadfastly hold onto it, particularly during challenging times. This is the only true way to see things from God's perspective. There are also some practical ways to put things into a positive perspective. Similar to boxing, winning a losing fight requires strategic thinking and adaptability. Here are five steps to improve your chances:

1. **Assess the Situation:** Take a moment to objectively evaluate the situation. Identify the key factors contributing to your disadvantage and understand the strengths and weaknesses of both sides.

2. **Adapt Your Strategy:** Recognize that your initial approach may not be working. Be willing to change tactics and adjust your strategy based on the evolving circumstances. If your current plan is not yielding positive results, it's essential to try something different.

3. **Exploit Weaknesses:** Analyze your opponent's vulnerabilities and capitalize on them. Every situation has its weak points, and finding and exploiting these weaknesses can turn the tide of the fight. This may involve targeting specific aspects of your opponent's strategy, skills, or resources that are less resilient.

4. **Stay Calm and Focused:** It's crucial to maintain composure even in challenging situations. Panic and frustration can cloud your judgment and hinder your ability to make strategic decisions. Stay

focused on your goals, remain calm, and think rationally to make the best choices under pressure.

5. **Utilize Creativity and Resourcefulness:** Think outside the box and use creative solutions to overcome obstacles. Consider unconventional approaches that others may not anticipate. Resourcefulness in adapting to the situation can provide you with unexpected advantages.

Winning a losing fight often involves a combination of mental toughness, strategic thinking, and adaptability. Each situation is unique, so it's important to assess and respond accordingly. Many accounts of Christ in the Word of God portray him as embodying a positive and compassionate perspective, even in the face of mistreatment. According to the New Testament, Jesus taught principles of love, forgiveness, and understanding. Here are a few examples that highlight his positive perspective:

Many accounts of Jesus in religious texts portray him as embodying a positive and compassionate perspective, even in the face of mistreatment. According to the New Testament of the Bible, Jesus taught principles of love, forgiveness, and understanding. Here are a few examples that highlight his positive perspective:

- **Love Your Enemies:** In the Sermon on the Mount **(Matthew 5:43-48)**, Jesus encourages his followers to love their enemies and pray for those who persecute them. This teaching emphasizes a perspective of compassion and forgiveness even toward those who may mistreat or oppose you.

- **Turn the Other Cheek:** Jesus is often quoted saying, **"But I tell you, do not resist an evil person. If anyone slaps you on the right cheek, turn to them the other cheek also"** (**Matthew 5:39**). This teaching suggests a non-retaliatory and peaceful response to mistreatment.

- **Forgiving Others:** Throughout the Gospels, Jesus emphasizes the importance of forgiveness. For example, in the Lord's Prayer, he includes the line *"Forgive us our debts, as we also have forgiven our debtors"* (**Matthew 6:12**), highlighting the reciprocal nature of forgiveness.

- **Compassion for Sinners:** Jesus was often seen associating with and showing compassion toward individuals considered sinners or outcasts in society. His interactions with tax collectors, prostitutes, and others demonstrated a perspective of love and acceptance rather than judgment.

- **Praying for Persecutors:** In one of his final moments on the cross, Jesus is depicted as praying for those who crucified him, saying, *"Father, forgive them, for they do not know what they are doing"* (**Luke 23:34**). This exemplifies a remarkable level of compassion and forgiveness even in the face of extreme suffering.

Therefore, we must have a totally different perspective about challenging times, mistreatment, or when being opposed. This mentality causes you to win no matter what because it is the mindset of one who has processed their fight ahead of time. Winning the battle with the proper perspective is the only option.

In the realm of experience, faith creates a space that enables a fresh perspective. It is important to ensure that your faith surpasses any doubt and unbelief. Doubt and unbelief will distort your perception and restrict your aspirations. Seek solace in the unknown and have unwavering faith that God can accomplish anything in your life without faltering and without fail.

I have learned to use my past and present experiences to be the launching pad for my future. How you handle past and present seasons will usually create the template and blueprint for the future. Do an assessment of your life and reroute your thoughts concerning experience to gain a different perspective concerning your life. I have not had the easiest life, nor do I have the perfect story. However, I do serve a master whose yoke is easy, and burdens are light. His story is perfect because He is a perfect God.

> *"Come to me, all you who are weary and burdened, and I will give you rest. Take my yoke upon you and learn from me, for I am gentle and humble in heart, and you will find rest for your souls. For my yoke is easy and my burden is light."*
> **Matthew 11:28-30**

I have developed the skill of preparing for the future by possessing the determination to consistently emerge as the victor. I have encountered numerous triumphs, which prevent me from being burdened by life's challenges. My foundation is rooted in faith, prayer, and trusting in God's process, regardless of appearances. My focus is solely on achieving victory and using it as a means to support others during their difficult times.

After facing my own personal struggles, I often come across individuals who are currently experiencing or recovering from similar situations. It is during these encounters that clarity emerges. I frequently discover the purpose behind my own hardships and how they have equipped me to provide solutions for others who find themselves in similar circumstances.

Regardless of one's background or origins, effectively navigating through life's various seasons is crucial to break free from repetitive cycles. The worst thing you can do during times of processing is miss the lesson that you were supposed to learn by reason of you being caught up in your emotions about the things you have deemed to be negative in your life.

There were certain challenges in my life that manifested as recurring events like horrifying anniversaries. I would express my desire for change verbally but faced difficulties in implementing it. However, once I shifted my outlook towards those encounters, I managed to overcome the negative aspects by applying the valuable yet initially uncomfortable lessons I had learned. Putting things in proper perspective will have a greater impact on your life and others, especially when you've applied the lessons learned. You are victorious!

CHAPTER
(Round 7)
CHOOSE YOUR CORNER WISELY

Life, similar to the sport of boxing, necessitates a strong support system. Having individuals in your life who can assist you in making prudent decisions, striking business deals, and navigating relationships is crucial. Making the right moves in life is essential for success and requires the skill of processing.

In boxing, this support system is referred to as "*Your Corner,*" while in life, it may be known as "*Your Support System.*" Regardless of the terminology, it is imperative to carefully select the individuals who will comprise your corner if you have any intentions of being victorious.

The individuals in the corner of a boxer during a match are typically referred to as the "**cornermen**" or "**corner team**." The key roles include:

- **Head Coach/Trainer:** The main coach responsible for overall strategy, training, and guiding the boxer during the fight.

- **Assistant Coach:** Assists the head coach and may focus on specific aspects of training or provide additional guidance during the match.

- **Cut man:** Responsible for treating any cuts or swelling on the boxer's face between rounds. They aim to minimize the impact of injuries on the boxer's performance.

- **Second/Cornerman:** Provides support, encouragement, and advice to the boxer during the fight. They may also assist with tasks like removing the boxer's mouthguard or applying ice.

These roles can vary, and some corner teams may include additional staff, such as a strength and conditioning coach. The composition of the corner team depends on the preferences of the boxer and their training camp.

The concept of a "corner team" extends beyond sports and can be applied to any collaborative effort where individuals work together with specific roles and responsibilities to achieve a common objective. Everyone needs a corner team. Moreover, the appropriate corner team.

A support system plays a crucial role in an individual's life by providing various forms of assistance, encouragement, and care. The responsibilities of a support system can encompass a wide range of aspects, depending on the needs and circumstances of the individual.

If the corner team of a boxer is not attentive or fails to perform their duties effectively, it can have significant consequences for the boxer's performance, health, and overall outcome of the match. The corner team plays a crucial role in providing support and guidance during breaks between rounds. Here are potential consequences of an inattentive corner team:

Missed Opportunities for Strategy Adjustments:
- Between rounds, the corner team assesses the opponent's tactics and the boxer's performance, providing strategic advice. If the team is not attentive, they may miss opportunities to adjust the game plan, potentially leading to a disadvantage in the next round.

Failure to Address Injuries or Swelling:
- The cut-man in the corner is responsible for treating any cuts or swelling on the boxer's face. If the corner team is not attentive, they may fail to address injuries promptly, increasing the risk of more severe damage and potentially leading to a referee stoppage.

Lack of Motivation and Encouragement:
- The corner team plays a crucial role in motivating and encouraging the boxer. If they are not attentive or fail to provide the necessary emotional support, the boxer's morale may suffer, impacting their performance in subsequent rounds.

Poor Physical and Mental Conditioning:
- Inattentiveness in the corner can lead to inadequate management of the boxer's physical and mental condition. This may result in fatigue, decreased focus, and diminished overall performance during the match.

Failure to Communicate Effectively:
- Communication between the boxer and the corner team is essential. If the team is not attentive or fails to communicate effectively, the boxer may not receive critical information or instructions, leading to

confusion and potential mistakes in the ring.

Increased Risk of Injury:
- Lack of attention to the boxer's condition and the opponent's strategy may increase the risk of injury. Inattentiveness can result in the boxer being ill-prepared to defend against specific tactics or being unable to adapt to the opponent's style.

Impact on Overall Match Outcome:
- The corner team plays a vital role in shaping the overall outcome of the match. Inattentiveness can contribute to a suboptimal performance by the boxer, potentially leading to a loss or a more challenging fight.

It's crucial for a corner team to be attentive, experienced, and well-prepared to handle various situations during a boxing match. Effective communication, strategic insight, and prompt attention to the boxer's physical condition are key elements of a successful corner team. Who do you have in your corner? Who's helping you make the right decision in your life? Have you chosen the right corner? What does your corner look like during challenges?

There may come times in your life when you must adapt your circle, particularly if you face continuous failure, lack of support, and destructive advice. It is crucial to have individuals who will speak the truth to you, even if you may not agree. The truth is what sets us free and shields us from defeat. Moreover, it empowers us to overcome defeat. With an honest circle, you can always find the strength to fight again and improve your performance in life.

In the sport of boxing, after a hard-fought match that ended in a loss, the corner gathers around the weary boxer in a somber yet supportive atmosphere. The head coach, with a mixture of empathy and constructive feedback, addresses the fighter. *"Hey champ, I know this didn't go the way we wanted, but let's talk about it. You showed incredible heart and determination in there. The opponent was tough, and we faced some unexpected challenges.*
We'll review the tape together and learn from this experience. There were moments of brilliance, and we'll build on those. Remember, every setback is a setup for a comeback. We'll go back to the gym, refine our strategy, and work on areas that need improvement. This is just one chapter in your journey, and we're in it together. Keep your head up; you're a fighter, and we'll come back stronger next time." The corner's discussion aims to balance acknowledgment of the difficulty with a forward-looking and motivational approach, fostering strength and growth for future matches.

I have carefully selected my incredible team. They provide guidance, feedback, viewpoints, and knowledge. Many of them possess expertise in specific fields, enabling me to achieve my objectives in the areas I have ventured into. A **Head Coach/Trainer** in my life would be my **Spiritual Father/Pastor:** *Dr. Rick Daniels* showcases love, training/instruction, discipleship, support, impartation, and aids me in achieving success in all aspects of life.

An **Assistant Coach in my life** would be my Mom *Karen Hoskins*: Mom has taught me all my life and has help me develop my relationship with Christ. She also gives me wisdom on making decisions in life, marriage, and anything in life. As it relates to a **Cut-man,** I actually have a host of individuals: These are individuals that I can depend on to help me deal with hurts, disappointment, breakdown, and even bad decisions. They provide me with wisdom on how to Responsible for properly recover from the bruises received in life during my journey. They aim to help me minimize the impact of injuries to succeed in all my endeavors.

A **Second/Cornerman** in my life would be: My Wife *Cheronda L. Hester* who Provides support, encouragement, and advice in everything that I do. She also assists with all my private disappointments. She helps me in removing my embarrassments, she helps me change my speech concerning moving forward, she prays constantly for me like applying ice. When it comes to my corner, my Wife *Cheronda L. Hester* truly plays a significant role in every aspect. We have faced numerous challenges, and she has stood by my side since the beginning. My Wife diligently prays for me, our family, and our church. I am immensely thankful to have such a supportive wife and friend who assists me in navigating through life's battles. I am absolutely certain that I would not have reached this point without her.

Every time I have to go to the emergency room, she sits huddled in the uncomfortable chairs, anxiously awaiting the results, while I lie in the hospital bed, filled with dread of receiving bad news or no solution at all.

Her support regarding my well-being is not just beneficial, but rather akin to the essential nourishment I require to maintain good health. Her words possess immense strength. My Wife has been solid as a rock during the times when I have felt shattered, and my spirit has been torn. However, my Wife provides me with a fresh view on relationships, situations, and even the overall perspective on life.

While penning down this book, I found myself engulfed in a whirlwind of depression, anxiety, stress, and fear simultaneously. As a pastor, I never anticipated being immersed in such depths of anguish, particularly after encountering numerous moments of triumph. Nevertheless, I had to bear in mind that Jesus himself endured certain trials, which should serve as a guiding light when we confront our own challenges in life.

Similar to boxing If the corner team that you have chosen to help you in life is not attentive or fails to perform their duties effectively, it can have significant consequences for your performance, health, and overall outcome of life. Your corner team plays a crucial role in providing support and guidance during challenges between seasons.

Here are potential consequences of an inattentive life corner team:

- **Missed Opportunities for Strategy Adjustments:** Certain seasons in life your corner team assesses the opponent's tactics and helps you to identify what's working against you in order to provide strategic advice. **If the team is not attentive, they may miss** opportunities to help you adjust your game plan, potentially leading to a disadvantage in the next season of life.

- **Failure to Address Injuries or Setbacks:** The cut-man in the corner of a boxer is responsible for treating any cuts or swelling on the boxer's face. In life **If the corner team is not attentive, they may fail at helping you to address some of life's injuries promptly, increasing the risk of more severe damage and potentially leading to a life of defeat.**

- **Lack of Motivation and Encouragement:** The corner team plays a crucial role in motivating and encouraging you through life to help you not quit. **If they are not attentive or fail to provide the necessary emotional support, your morale may suffer, impacting your ability to perform in subsequent seasons of life.**

- **Poor Physical and Mental Conditioning:** Inattentiveness in the corner can lead to inadequate management of your physical and mental condition. **This may result in fatigue, decreased focus, and diminished overall performance during certain seasons in life.** You need mentally healthy people in your corner. This is very important.

- **Failure to Communicate Effectively:** Communication between you and the corner team is essential. If the team is not attentive or fails to communicate effectively, you may not receive critical information or instructions, leading to confusion and potential mistakes during your pursuit of victory. You can lose in life because of confusion between you and those you trust. **1 Corinthians 15:33** *Evil communication corrupts good manners.*

- **Increased Risk of Injury:** Lack of attention to your condition and the lack of ability to help you identify the obstacles ahead may increase the risk of injury. Inattentiveness can result in you being ill-prepared to defend against specific tactics or being unable to adapt to the challenges of life. **There is no defeat quite as crushing as the defeat you encounter when you have relied on someone to aid you in addressing a problem, only to find yourself sinking deeper into despair.**

- **Impact on Overall Match Outcome:** The corner team plays a vital role in shaping the overall outcome of the journey you are taking in life. Inattentiveness may result in a poor pursuit of victory, which could potentially lead to a defeat or more difficult days ahead.

When you are part of someone's support system, it is important to avoid adding more darkness or unresolved chaos to your own life. By doing so, you risk extinguishing the light in the life of the person you should be assisting in overcoming their struggles.

During my less experienced days as a pastor, I have regrettably allowed darkness to overshadow my own life, resulting in the defeat of others and my failure to fulfill my role in their lives. It is truly disheartening to carry the burden of disappointment as both a leader and a trusted individual.

Many are experiencing defeat in various aspects of their lives, such as battles, opportunities, significant deals, marriages, and even failing their children. This is primarily due to the presence of having the wrong people in their corner. You must understand that not everyone should have access to you or be involved in your endeavors, especially when you are striving for success in all areas of life.

God can help you in choosing the right people in your life. Try seeking God through prayer, meditation, or the study of His Word to discern the right path or make decisions about relationships. I believe that God provides guidance through inner feelings, intuition, or a sense of conviction especially when you are following His spirit. Be sure to pray for wisdom and discernment to make choices aligned with Gods spiritual values.

CHAPTER
(Round 8)
A WARRIOR'S MENTALITY

A warrior's mindset is frequently connected with an attitude that highlights power, endurance, self-control, and resolve. Although the term "*warrior*" is typically associated with military situations, it has also been embraced in a wider sense to depict individuals who confront challenges with a concentrated and disciplined mindset.

There are several essential attributes often linked to a warrior's mentality.

- **Courage:** "Be strong and courageous. Do not be afraid; do not be discouraged, for the Lord your God will be with you wherever you go." *(Joshua 1:9)*

- **Discipline:** "But I discipline my body and keep it under control, lest after preaching to others I myself should be disqualified." *(1 Corinthians 9:27)*

- **Perseverance:** "Blessed is the one who perseveres under trial because, having stood the test, that person will receive the crown of life that the Lord has promised to those who love him." *(James 1:12)*

- **Focus:** "But one thing I do: forgetting what lies behind and straining forward to what lies ahead, I press on toward the goal for the prize of the upward call of God in Christ Jesus."

(Philippians 3:13-14)

- **Adaptability:** "For I know the plans I have for you, declares the Lord, plans for welfare and not for evil, to give you a future and a hope." *(Jeremiah 29:11)*

- **Loyalty:** "Let love and faithfulness never leave you; bind them around your neck, write them on the tablet of your heart." *(Proverbs 3:3)*

- **Integrity:** "The integrity of the upright guides them, but the unfaithful are destroyed by their duplicity." *(Proverbs 11:3)*

- **Leadership:** "But among you it will be different. Whoever wants to be a leader among you must be your servant." *(Mark 10:43)*

These scriptures provide biblical insights into attributes like bravery, self-control, perseverance, concentration, flexibility, faithfulness, honesty, and guidance that are frequently linked with the mindset of a warrior.

ENDURING THE HARDEST TIMES

I have had to employ all these qualities at some point in my life and often I have not always implemented them immediately. This is why it is extremely important to always stay connected to individuals who possess wisdom and greater life experience than you. I understand that many of you have faced intense battles within your own minds. Perhaps you have experienced some truly devastating events in your life, and you may be questioning how you managed to overcome them. It was the warrior's mentality within you that enabled you to endure and find strength in the things that truly matter, leading you towards victory on the other side of your struggles.

It took a warrior's mentality to overcome the death of my Brother *Juawaun D. Hester Sr*. I still can't tell you how I managed to eulogize him and watch him be lowered into his grave. It was the same with my Aunt *Monica Stamps*. God gave me the strength, the focus, and the ability to be strong for my family as I officiated their services. These were two of the most devastating times in life, but I had courage and adapted to lead my family to a space of peace the best I knew how.

Overcoming the loss of my Brother *Juawaun D. Hester Sr.* and my Aunt *Monica Stamps* required a warrior's mentality. Reflecting on how I managed to deliver their eulogies and witness their burial still leaves me in awe. With God's grace, I found the strength, determination, and perseverance to support my family during their services. Although these were incredibly challenging moments, I had courage to adapt and lead my loved ones towards finding peace in the best way I could.

It took a warrior's mentality to endure those four months living in the hotel unsure if we would ever buy our home. We battled through sickness, depression, despair and came out victorious. The place of prayer is all we had along with our faith. During your most difficult times in life, you must believe that God will hear you and answer you when you pray.
*"Then you will **call on me** and **come and pray to me**, and*

<u>*I will listen to you.*</u>"
Jeremiah 29:12

*"This is the confidence we have in approaching God: that **if we ask anything** according to his will, **he hears us**. And if <u>we know</u> that he hears us—<u>**whatever we ask**</u>—we know that <u>**we have what we asked of him.**</u>"*
1 John 5:14-15

Living in the **Cabrini Green Projects**, my mother exemplified a warrior's mentality. My aunt *Beverly Ann Moore* battled breast cancer, but sadly, we lost her to the disease. She had six children, who overnight became my brother and sisters. In a remarkable display of strength, my mother brought together her three children and my six cousins, creating a united family under one roof in our project apartment.

My Mother taught us about building a relationship with Christ. She also demonstrated the true essence of constructing a life without relying on excuses. Her unwavering display of support, love, and understanding was truly remarkable. Despite the immense challenges, the perilous environment, and the most dangerous place to live in Chicago during that period, she remained steadfast.

PRINCIPLES TO LIVING WITH A WARRIOR'S MENTALITY

In the vast tapestry of existence, those who are like warriors are distinguished not only by their prowess in combat but, perhaps more significantly, by their unwavering spirit and refusal to surrender in the face of adversity. When you must live like a warrior you have an unconquerable mindset of never backing down, showcasing the principles and practices that ignite your determination.

The Warrior Mentality: Warriors approach challenges with a distinct mindset—a blend of discipline, bravery, and unwavering determination. Your mind is finely attuned to perceive obstacles not as insurmountable barriers but as opportunities for growth and triumph. Embracing the warrior mentality means confronting adversity head-on, armed with the belief that every struggle is a step towards personal and collective victory.

Faith in the Face of Defeat: As a warrior you must comprehend that defeat is not the end but a temporary setback. Instead of succumbing to despair, you utilize setbacks as catalysts for improvement. Resilience forms the foundation of your character, enabling you to bounce back stronger, wiser, and more prepared for future challenges. In the warrior's realm, every defeat is a summons to rise again, even more formidable than before.

Perseverance Amidst Pain: Warriors acknowledge that the path to success is often paved with pain and hardship. You embrace discomfort and endure adversities, recognizing that enduring temporary pain can lead to enduring glory. Perseverance acts as the warrior's shield against the wear and tear of life's battles, providing the strength to push through when others may falter.

Devotion to a Cause: What will set you apart is your unwavering devotion to a cause greater than yourself. Whether it be personal growth, the protection of loved ones, or a higher purpose, as a warrior you draw strength from your dedication. This commitment fuels your determination and serves as a constant reminder that surrender is never an option.

Learning from Every Encounter: Every battle, regardless of the outcome, serves as a wellspring of valuable lessons for those with a warrior's mindset. You meticulously analyze each engagement, extracting wisdom and insights. These lessons become the building blocks of your growth and evolution, propelling you towards greater heights.

As Warriors, we never give up but rather we embody a spirit that transcends the battlefield. Your perseverance, and commitment to a cause serve as inspiration for anyone navigating the complexities of life. You become an example of strength even though you feel weak, broken and defeated at times. By adopting the warrior mentality, we can find the strength to face our own challenges, knowing that within us lies the unyielding spirit that never surrenders, no matter how fierce the battle.

Embracing the Warrior Within
Ultimately, the spirit of warriors who never give up resides within everyone. It's a mindset that can be cultivated through discipline, self-reflection, and a commitment to personal growth. Embracing the warrior within means acknowledging one's own strength,

facing challenges with courage, and persisting in the pursuit of noble goals.

Encountering Fear with Courage: Fear is a natural companion on this journey, but instead of allowing it to paralyze you, warriors face fear with courage. You must understand that true bravery is not the absence of fear but the ability to act in its presence. By confronting your fears head-on, you demonstrate a strength that goes beyond physical expertise—it is the strength of character that refuses to be subdued.

When Christ lives on the inside of you, you have greatness on the inside of you. You can do all things through Christ *Philippians 4:13.* In addition, God has not given you the spirit of fear so continue to walk in faith and believe that victory belongs to you. There will be days when you are forced to live with no other mindset but a warrior. Backed into a corner with no other choice but to fight your way out until you realize that there is a strength in you that was waiting to be discovered, activated and trusted!

OVERCOMING AXIETY WITH A WARRIOR'S MENTALITY

During the process of writing this book, there were moments when anxiety and stress reached their peak. There were instances when I contemplated giving up on everything due to the overwhelming challenges that came my way. However, I had numerous reasons to refrain. God bestowed upon me the fortitude, the faith, and the support required to continue as a warrior.

There will be times in life when things are similar to a boxing match. You will feel as if you are losing it all. Losing every round and emotionally drained. Being determined to not quit is the only mindset to have during tough times. Ultimately, you will need to live life with extreme faith that no matter how things look, believe that God will give you the victory.

I have witnessed boxers engaging in bouts, enduring blood, scars, and facial disfigurement, yet emerging victorious. If you can endure the agony and maintain your determination, there is a possibility of triumphing in life's challenging moments. I urge you to persist in your fight until you witness your own triumph. I firmly believe that there exists a warrior within everyone, particularly if your body instinctively knows how to activate its fight or flight response. By nature, you were designed to survive and shield yourself from defeat.

Be the person who never accepts defeat. Be the kind of individual who struggles to give up. Be the fighter who persists until triumph is achieved in all aspects of your struggles. Embrace obstacles, even invite them, and let them mold you into the best version of yourself. Keep striving, persevering, and remaining productive regardless of the circumstances.

The more you process your thoughts, experiences, and challenges the easier you find it to maintain a warrior's mindset. I often tell myself, "You can do this, and you have seen victory in areas like this before." Overall, I *can do all things through Christ who strengthens me!* **Philippians 4:13**

I have come to a stage in my life where I am compelled to embrace a life guided solely by faith. Without Faith it is impossible to please God. Faith has the power to alleviate the anguishes in life. A person who possesses unwavering faith is a warrior who fears nothing except the Lord. When we live by faith, we can overcome trials that have claimed the lives of others. Life tends to transform individuals into warriors, particularly if you process life and its obstacles properly. Victory will always be your companion, even in moments of apparent defeat.

STAYING MOTIVATED WITH A WARRIOR'S MENTALITY

Staying motivated can be achieved by constantly reminding ourselves of the promises God has made for our lives. I firmly believe that to conquer challenges and achieve success, it is essential for every individual to remain connected to their divine purpose. If we allow ourselves to be distracted, we are essentially surrendering to defeat, especially if we lack that spiritual connection. The adversary seeks to make us succumb to the difficult phases of life, but we must resist. Instead, we should adjust our focus and realign ourselves with the principles, core values, and instructions that God has already bestowed upon us through His word.

Here are three principles to help maintain motivation during difficult circumstances:

Focus on Purpose and Meaning:
Principle: Remind yourself of your overarching

purpose and the meaning behind your goals, values, and aspirations. Connect with the deeper reasons why you started on your journey, and how persevering through challenges aligns with your core values.
- **Romans 5:3-4 -** *"Not only so, but we also glory in our sufferings, because we know that suffering produces perseverance; perseverance, character; and character, hope."*
- **Philippians 3:13-14 -** *"Brothers and sisters, I do not consider myself yet to have taken hold of it. But one thing I do: Forgetting what is behind and straining toward what is ahead, I press on toward the goal to win the prize for which God has called me heavenward in Christ Jesus."*

Seek Support and Community:
Principle: Build a strong network of supportive individuals, including friends, family, mentors, or like-minded individuals, who can provide you with encouragement, understanding, and practical help when facing challenges. Be open about your struggles and seek advice from those who can offer valuable insights and a fresh perspective. Be sure to seek help from the right individuals.
- **Ecclesiastes 4:9-10 -** *"Two are better than one, because they have a good return for their labor: If either of them falls down, one can help the other up. But pity anyone who falls and has no one to help them up."*
- **Galatians 6:2 -** *"Carry each other's burdens, and in this way you will fulfill the law of Christ.*

Practice Self-Compassion and Resilience:
Principle: During challenging moments, it is crucial to nurture self-compassion by treating oneself with kindness, understanding, and patience. It is important to acknowledge that setbacks and obstacles are

inevitable in life, and by embracing them, one can develop resilience and adaptability.
- **Psalm 34:18** - *"The LORD is close to the brokenhearted and saves those who are crushed in spirit."*
- **James 1:2-4** - *"Consider it pure joy, my brothers and sisters, whenever you face trials of many kinds, because you know that the testing of your faith produces perseverance. Let perseverance finish its work so that you may be mature and complete, not lacking anything."*

By grounding yourself in your purpose and finding meaning, reaching out for support from a community, and cultivating self-compassion and resilience, you can maintain your motivation and resilience even in the face of incredibly challenging circumstances. As a result, you will emerge from these difficult times stronger and more determined to conquer any adversity that comes your way.

One of the worst things you can do in life is give up and quit before putting up an aggressive fight. Utilizing prayer, faith, and prophetic ministry will also help you to not just overcome but to maximize your edge and manifest your purpose in God despite what you're facing. Get up out of your corner of defeat and get back in the fight, it is not over yet!

Giving up and quitting before putting up a fierce fight is one of the most detrimental actions one can take in life. By incorporating prayer, faith, and prophetic ministry, you can not only conquer obstacles but also enhance your advantage and fulfill your divine purpose, regardless of the challenges you encounter. Rise from the depths of defeat and rejoin the battle, for it is far from being concluded! Get up out of your corner of defeat and get back in the fight, it is not over yet!

After every bell rings, a boxer retreats to their corner, knowing that their success hinges on the guidance they will receive from their corner and their ability to adapt and employ their skills to overcome their opponent. Now, it is your turn to do the exact same thing. Embrace this moment to uncover the realities about your corner, your abilities, and the challenges you face. Process the fight!

CHAPTER
(Round 9)
HOW TO WIN WHEN YOU HAVE LOST

This chapter may not prove advantageous to all individuals unless one possesses an open-minded attitude and a genuine eagerness to acquire knowledge on effectively handling a situation where victory seems unlikely. In my previous discussions, I have often made use of boxing as an analogy to aid in comprehending the subject matter better. However, this chapter will primarily cater to those who are willing to explore a more spiritual perspective, as everything originates from the realm of the spirit.

Utilizing prayer, intercession, the prophetic ministry, and the power in the name Jesus Christ's are key strategies to achieve victory even in the face of defeat. These powerful dynamics have been my source of strength during the most challenging moments of my life.

UTILIZING PRAYER/INTERCESSION TO WIN

Prayer and intercession are closely related concepts within the realm of spiritual practice, but they have distinct meanings and purposes:

Prayer is a broad term that encompasses communication with God in the context of our faith.
- It involves various forms of communication, such as worship, thanksgiving, confession, supplication, and petition.

- Prayer can be individual or communal and may involve speaking, listening, or contemplation.
- In prayer, individuals express their thoughts, feelings, desires, and concerns to God, seeking spiritual connection, guidance, comfort, and blessings.

Intercession:
- Intercession refers specifically to a form of prayer where one person (the intercessor) petitions or pleads on behalf of another individual, group, or situation.
- Intercession involves advocating for others before God, often with a focus on their needs, challenges, or well-being.
- Intercessory prayer may include requests for healing, protection, provision, reconciliation, or spiritual growth on behalf of others.
- Intercessors act as mediators between God and those they are praying for, bringing their concerns before the divine and seeking divine intervention or assistance on their behalf.

Several figures in the Bible turned to prayer to seek victory in battles or conflicts. Here are a few notable examples:

Joshua: In the book of Joshua, we see Joshua leading the Israelites into the Promised Land, facing numerous battles along the way. Before the battle of Jericho, Joshua prayed and sought instructions from the Lord. Following God's instructions, the Israelites marched around the city walls, and on the seventh day, after the seventh procession, the walls of Jericho collapsed, leading to victory for the Israelites (**Joshua 6**).

King Jehoshaphat: When the kingdom of Judah faced invasion from a coalition of enemies, King Jehoshaphat called the people to fast and pray. He led a prayer before the assembly, acknowledging their dependence on God for deliverance. In response, God assured them of victory, and they were supernaturally delivered without even having to fight. The enemy forces turned on each other, resulting in the defeat of Judah's enemies (**2 Chronicles 20**).

King Hezekiah When the Assyrian king Sennacherib threatened to attack Jerusalem, King Hezekiah prayed earnestly for deliverance. He spread Sennacherib's threatening letter before the Lord in the temple and pleaded for God's intervention. In response, God sent an angel who struck down the Assyrian army, saving Jerusalem from destruction (**2 Kings 19, 2 Chronicles 32**).

David: Throughout his life, David faced numerous battles and challenges. He often turned to prayer for strength, guidance, and victory. In many of the Psalms attributed to David, we see him pouring out his heart to God, seeking refuge, deliverance, and triumph over his enemies. Psalm 18, for example, recounts David's gratitude to God for delivering him from the hand of Saul and other adversaries.

These biblical examples demonstrate the power of prayer in times of conflict and the importance of relying on God for strength, wisdom, and victory in battles. Whether facing physical enemies or spiritual challenges, prayer served as a crucial weapon for these individuals in securing God's help and deliverance.

The Word of God inspires us to pray continuously and emphasizes the importance of consistent prayer. It is not a sporadic activity but rather a regular practice, especially considering the constant attacks from the adversary.

UTILIZING THE PROPHETIC REALM TO WIN

The heart, will, and counsel of God encompass the prophetic. Gaining access to it necessitates an understanding of the spiritual realm. God communicates with us through His prophets and His Word. When He speaks through individuals, it is known as a "Rhema Word," which in Greek signifies an "utterance" or "thing said." On the other hand, when He speaks through His Word, it is referred to as the "Logos Word." The term "Logos" pertains to the written facts that substantiate what is spoken.

In the Word of God, prophecy was frequently utilized as a method of divine communication to provide guidance to individuals, communities, and nations in various aspects of life. There are several ways in which prophecy was employed to assist in life. To begin with, prophets were frequently called upon to foretell future events, such as disasters, wars, or impending judgments. Notable prophets like Isaiah, Jeremiah, and Ezekiel warned the Israelites about the consequences of their disobedience and predicted the destruction of Jerusalem by foreign powers.

Moreover, prophecy offered divine guidance and direction to individuals and leaders who faced important decisions. Kings and rulers sought the counsel of prophets to discern God's will in matters of governance, warfare, and alliances. For instance, King David sought guidance from the prophet Nathan, while King Hezekiah turned to the prophet Isaiah during times of crisis.

Prophets also delivered messages calling people to repentance and spiritual renewal. They rebuked moral and religious corruption and urged individuals and nations to turn back to God. A remarkable example of prophecy leading to widespread spiritual transformation is the prophet Jonah's message of repentance to the city of Nineveh.

Furthermore, prophecy provided encouragement, consolation, and hope to individuals and communities facing adversity. Prophets delivered messages of comfort and assurance, promising God's presence, and eventual deliverance. The book of Isaiah contains numerous prophecies of comfort and restoration for the Israelites during times of exile and hardship.

Additionally, prophecy served to confirm God's promises and covenants with His people. Through the prophets, God reaffirmed His faithfulness and reminded the Israelites of His enduring love and commitment to them. Prophecies regarding the coming Messiah, found in books like Micah and Isaiah, reinforced the hope of salvation and redemption.

PERSONAL PROPHETIC COUNSEL

Throughout my journey, I've encountered numerous instances where a prophetic word has come to my rescue. We are living a prophetic life which requires prophetic influence and counsel. I am a firm believer that the prophetic is a necessity to make it through life.

Prophecy can foretell impending danger or calamity, providing an opportunity to take preventive action. Just as prophets in the Bible warned of imminent threats, modern- day prophecy can alert individuals and communities to potential dangers, allowing them to prepare and take necessary precautions.

Prophetic counsel can offer divine guidance and direction in decision-making and life choices. When faced with uncertainty or difficult circumstances, prophetic messages can provide clarity and insight into God's will, helping individuals navigate their paths with confidence and wisdom.

Prophetic counsel can bring encouragement and comfort to those facing trials, hardships, or emotional distress. Through prophetic words of affirmation, assurance, and hope, individuals can find strength and solace in the midst of adversity, knowing that God is with them and has a plan for their lives.

Prophetic counsel can serve as a call to repentance and spiritual renewal, rescuing individuals from the destructive paths of sin and disobedience. Prophetic messages of conviction and correction prompt hearts to turn back to God, leading to forgiveness, reconciliation, and restoration of relationships with Him.

Prophetic counsel reveals God's promises and faithfulness to His people, reminding them of His love, provision, and faithfulness. Through prophetic utterances, individuals are reminded of God's covenant promises and encouraged to trust in His faithfulness, even amid trials and tribulations.

Prophetic counsel can confirm individuals' identities and purposes in God's kingdom, affirming their unique gifts, callings, and destinies. By receiving prophetic words that align with God's plans and purposes for their lives, individuals are empowered to step into their God-given roles with confidence and boldness.

Prophecy can release supernatural provision, protection, and intervention in times of need. Through prophetic declarations and prayers, individuals can activate God's power and authority to overcome obstacles, defeat enemies, and experience divine breakthroughs in their lives.

Prophecy played a vital role in leading individuals, communities, and nations in the Bible. It provided forewarnings, divine insight, calls to repentance, encouragement, and confirmation of God's promises.

PROPHETIC DREAMS

Dreams that are believed to predict future events or provide insights into important aspects of one's life or the world around them are known as prophetic dreams. These dreams are thought to offer glimpses into the future or serve as warnings or insight from God, the subconscious mind, or other sources like the flesh realm.

Throughout history and across different cultures, there have been numerous accounts of individuals claiming to have experienced prophetic dreams that accurately foretold future events. These events can vary from personal occurrences, such as the loss of a loved one or a significant life change, to more global events or natural disasters.

Prophetic dreams have captivated the interest of psychologists, spiritual leaders, and scholars, who have studied them extensively. While some people dismiss these dreams as mere coincidences or the result of subconscious information processing, others believe in their potential to reveal profound truths about the nature of reality and human existence.

It's important to understand that the interpretation of dreams, including prophetic ones, can be highly subjective and influenced by cultural, religious, and personal beliefs.
Therefore, what may be considered a prophetic dream by one person may not hold the same significance for another. In addition, every dream is not a prophetic dream. In the Word of God, there are numerous instances of dreams and dreamers that hold great significance. Here are a couple of examples:

Joseph, son of Jacob (*Genesis 37-50*): Joseph, the son of Jacob (also known as Israel), is widely recognized as one of the most prominent dreamers in the Bible. He had two prophetic dreams where he saw himself ruling over his family. These dreams, combined with his coat of many colors, sparked jealousy among his brothers, leading them to sell him into slavery in Egypt. However, Joseph's remarkable ability to interpret dreams eventually elevated him to a position of power in Egypt. He played a crucial role in helping Pharaoh interpret his own prophetic dreams about an upcoming famine.

Pharaoh's Dreams (*Genesis 41*): Pharaoh, the ruler of Egypt, experienced two significant dreams that deeply troubled him. In the first dream, he witnessed seven healthy cows being devoured by seven sickly cows. In the second dream, he saw seven full ears of grain being consumed by seven thin and blighted ears.

None of Pharaoh's wise men could decipher the meaning behind these dreams. However, Joseph, who was imprisoned at the time, was brought before Pharaoh and successfully interpreted the dreams as a prediction of seven years of abundance followed by seven years of famine. Impressed by Joseph's interpretation, Pharaoh appointed him as second in command over Egypt.

Daniel: Daniel, a Hebrew prophet, possessed the extraordinary ability to interpret dreams, which played a significant role in the Book of Daniel. One notable instance is when King Nebuchadnezzar of Babylon had a troubling dream that none of his wise men could decipher. However, Daniel was able to interpret the dream, which revealed the rise and fall of various kingdoms, including Babylon itself.

These examples merely scratch the surface of the biblical dreamers and their dreams. Dreams hold a profound significance in the narrative of the Word of God, often serving as a means through which divine messages or guidance are conveyed to individuals or rulers. Ultimately, the key to living a triumphant life lies in our ability to discern God's voice amidst difficult circumstances. The prophetic ministry is not limited to the confines of a church; it is a vital necessity.

KINGS AND PROPHETS

In ancient times, prophets were appointed to assist kings in governing wisely. Similarly, our present-day leaders require the assistance of prophets and prophetic voices to govern effectively. Likewise, each of us needs the prophetic in our lives to govern ourselves wisely.

In the Bible, there were several instances where prophets played a significant role in assisting kings. One such example is Samuel, who anointed Saul as the first king of Israel as per God's command. Samuel continued to guide Saul throughout his reign, but Saul's disobedience led to God rejecting him as king. Samuel was then instructed to anoint David as Saul's successor.

Similarly, Nathan was a prophet during King David's reign. He confronted David about his sins and provided counsel and guidance. Nathan also played a role in Solomon's accession to the throne and offered him messages from God. Elijah and Elisha were prophets who challenged the wickedness of King Ahab and his wife Jezebel, while Isaiah provided counsel and reassurance to King Hezekiah during times of crisis. Prophets played a crucial role in advising kings, delivering divine messages, and calling for repentance and obedience.

LIVING A PROPHETIC LIFE

Life can be a complex journey if you lack the ability to navigate, resources, and a connection with God. I am determined to live my life solely based on God's instructions, revelations, and His presence. Without God, it is like a fish trying to survive outside of water.

Life is predetermined and should be lived in accordance with a specific set of principles to fulfill God's expectations, as He is the creator of life. Although things may not always be flawless or effortless, aligning yourself with God's plans and purposes will bring you the ultimate reward.

I heard the voice of God instruct me to plant our Church. I heard His voice tell me what our church name should be. I have also been the conduit in the lives of so many others as that prophetic voice as a prophet of God myself. However, I am not exempt from the results of not listening to the voice of God.

I have also heard the voice of God when attempting to do things of my own knowledge, fleshly desires, and on my own strength only to come up in places of pain, struggle or even broken. So, I have experienced a well-rounded experience when it comes to prophetic ministry. You definitely do not want to create a cycle of not listening to God's voice when He speaks because ignoring Him never turns out well.

I have been privileged to hear the voice of God speak to me about establishing our Church. His voice also revealed to me the perfect name for our congregation. As a prophet of God, I have served as a conduit for His prophetic voice, impacting the lives of many others. However, I must acknowledge that even as a prophet, I am not exempt of the consequences of disregarding God's voice.

On a personal level, I have also encountered instances where I relied solely on my own understanding, worldly desires, and or personal strength, only to find myself in situations of pain, struggle, and brokenness. Through these experiences, I have gained a comprehensive understanding of prophetic ministry. It is crucial to avoid falling into a pattern of ignoring God's voice, as the outcome is never favorable.

The ability to discern and know God's voice for oneself is considered essential for spiritual well-being and fulfillment. It involves a process of prayer, reflection, study, and openness to the workings of His power in your life. It is my prayer that you be connected to the right prophetic people, cultures, communities and or churches to get the best out of life.

It is important to note that some individuals do not believe that there are potential dangers connected to not having a prophetic experience. This though is not universal. Many can live an upright life regardless of their beliefs about the prophetic. However, for those who derive insight, guidance and meaning from prophetic teachings, living without them may present certain challenges that require thoughtful consideration and adaptation.

I believe as they did in the Word of God. It is my desire for all believers to prophesy and live prophetic lives. I also believe this idea is supported by several scriptures, particularly in the New Testament. Here are a few passages that highlight this concept:

- **1 Corinthians 14:1-5 (NIV):** "Follow the way of love and eagerly desire gifts of the Spirit, especially prophecy. For anyone who speaks in a tongue does not speak to people but to God. Indeed, no one understands them; they utter mysteries by the Spirit. But the one who prophesies speaks to people for their strengthening, encouraging and comfort. Anyone who speaks in a tongue edifies themselves, but the one who prophesies edifies the church. I would like every one of you to speak in tongues, but **I would rather have you prophesy.** The one who prophesies is greater than the one who speaks in tongues, unless someone interprets, so that the church may be edified."

- **Acts 2:17-18 (NIV):** "'In the last days, God says, I will pour out my Spirit on all people. Your sons and daughters will prophesy, your young men will see visions, your old men will dream dreams. Even on my servants, both men and women, I will pour out my Spirit in those days, and they will prophesy.'"

- **1 Thessalonians 5:19-21 (NIV):** "Do not quench the Spirit. Do not treat prophecies with contempt but test them all; hold on to what is good."

- **Joel 2:28-29 (NIV):** "'And afterward, I will pour out my Spirit on all people. Your sons and daughters will prophesy, your old men will dream dreams, your young men will see visions. Even on my servants, both men and women, I will pour out my Spirit in those days.'"

These verses emphasize the importance of desiring spiritual gifts, especially the gift of prophecy, and they suggest that this gift is not limited to a select few but is available to all believers. The purpose of prophecy is seen as edification, encouragement, and comfort for the church community. Additionally, the passages from Acts and Joel suggest that the outpouring of the Holy Spirit enables believers of all ages and backgrounds to prophesy, indicating inclusivity within the body of Christ.

UNDERSTANDING THE POWER IN MASTERING TIME TO WIN

Some boxers in the sport of boxing are known for their exceptional power punches. Despite lacking in footwork, skills, or top-notch training, these fighters have the ability to knock out their opponents with just one punch.

Certain life experiences can create a sense of being trapped in an un-winnable struggle. In such moments, the significance of timing cannot be overstated. A skilled boxer harnesses their mastery of time to deliver powerful punches. The key factor in such situations is the cultivation of patience. I had to acquire this skill to avoid prematurely ending certain phases of life.

Jesus is the ultimate authority over power and time. If you need development in this realm, He possesses an unparalleled track record of effectively managing power and time simultaneously. There is much wisdom to be gained from Jesus to achieve success through the strategic utilization of power and time.

Jesus frequently highlighted the significance of aligning one's life with God's plan in the here and now. His teachings centered around principles like *forgiveness, love,* and *compassion,* underscoring the value of how people choose to allocate their time and assets.

As believers we believe Jesus' life, ministry, death, and resurrection were all seen as occurring at precisely the right moments in accordance with God's plan for humanity's salvation. This divine timing is often emphasized in the New Testament, with passages such as **Galatians 4:4** stating that Jesus came into the world *"in the fullness of time."*

Jesus performed various miracles that transcended natural limitations, including healing the sick, raising the dead, and multiplying food. These acts were not just displays of power but also demonstrations of Jesus' authority over the natural order, suggesting a supernatural understanding of time and its constraints.

Jesus often spoke about the significance of time in his teachings. For example, he urged his followers to prioritize spiritual matters and to live in the present moment, rather than worrying excessively about the future (**Matthew 6:25-34**). His teachings emphasized the importance of using time wisely and being prepared for the eventual return of the Son of Man.

From an eternal perspective, Jesus frequently spoke about eternal life and the kingdom of God, emphasizing a perspective that transcends temporal concerns. For believers, Jesus' victory over sin and death offers the promise of eternal life beyond the constraints of earthly time.

Although the primary understanding of Jesus' control over time lies in his divine nature and mission, his teachings and deeds serve as a constant source of inspiration for believers to reflect upon the importance of time in their personal lives and spiritual quests.

There is power in being patient knowing the right time to do a thing or to not move on it. The victory is not in how well you perform in life but in how well you wait to be led by God. Time can always be on your side when you allow the example of Jesus to be your template for becoming victorious in your life.

Christ is the greatest example of what it looks like to win while losing. Having Him as the head of your lead and literally submitting to Him is the only way to accomplish your goals and purpose in life. He becomes your strength during those tough seasons, especially the ones that are too much to endure.

PUSHING THROUGH YOUR LOSS TO DISCOVER YOUR WIN

During the process of writing this book, I faced some of the most difficult times in my life. I persisted in applying the principles I have shared, but I must admit that there were moments when I felt utterly alone, abandoned by God, and even defeated, despite knowing deep down that it wasn't true. I struggled with unhealthy thoughts and fought to maintain my sanity.

One particular day, I woke up with heavy thoughts of suicide weighing on my mind. I engaged in a mental battle unlike any I had experienced before, with satan's influence strongly felt. My mind would often be consumed by draining, nauseating thoughts and migraines. I came close to giving up on everything.

On a personal level, I found myself breaking down in tears during business meetings, unable to pinpoint the source of my inner turmoil. Nevertheless, I continued to fulfill my responsibilities of preaching and pastoring God's people. It was during this time that I recognized the divine promotion at hand, understanding that I was paying a price for reaching a new level.

Upon realizing the different shifts in my personal life, I was able to embrace the process that I was going through. With our home up for foreclosure, cars on the repossession list and constant visits to the hospital emergency room, I still found joy in serving God's people and appreciating life with my family. I was being molded into a new person, new leader, new Father, and new Husband.

Overcoming loss to find your victory requires patience, growth, and self-discovery. Here's a guide to help you along the way:

- Give yourself the space to acknowledge and process the loss you've faced. Whether it's a job, a relationship, or something else significant, it s important to confront your emotions and accept the reality of the situation. Allow yourself to feel the sadness, anger, and disappointment that may arise, as these emotions are a natural part of the healing process. I found that focusing on healing and growth, rather than fighting my emotions, was key to moving forward and becoming a better version of myself.

- Avoid dwelling on negative emotions. Instead, focus on finding joy and strength in your journey towards healing. Seek support from those who care about you, as their perspective and guidance can be invaluable during this time.

- Reflect on the circumstances that led to your loss and consider what lessons you can learn from the experience. By examining your actions and choices, you can gain valuable insights that will help you in the future. I realized that addressing my emotional decisions was crucial for my well-being and personal growth.

- Once you have processed your emotions and gained clarity, set new goals for yourself, and take proactive steps towards achieving them. Focus on what you can control and project your energy into positive actions that will lay the groundwork for your future success. One of the things I had to do is Return to my previous company, where I found success and clarity. It was a pivotal moment for me. I was able to reconcile relationships, reconcile with my stream of success and with my former business partners.

- Setbacks are an inevitable part of any journey towards success. It is crucial to remain determined and patient in the face of adversity, refusing to let temporary defeats discourage you from pursuing your goals. Any fighter will attest that a loss is merely an opportunity to keep fighting until victory is achieved.

- Moreover, it is essential to acknowledge and celebrate the small victories along the way. Celebrate the progress you have made and trust that life will continue to improve from here. Each step forward, regardless of its size, brings you closer to your ultimate triumph. I had to awaken from my slumber and put in the necessary effort to witness the victory that God had already planned. It is crucial to detach yourself from your previous level, taking only the lessons learned and leaving everything else behind.

- Instead of viewing a loss as a setback, consider it an opportunity for personal growth and development. Utilize it as fuel to propel yourself forward and become the best version of yourself. Keep pushing forward, even when faced with challenges. Remember that perseverance is the key to overcoming obstacles and achieving success.

- Discovering your win is a personal journey that is unique to you. Be patient with yourself, remain committed to your goals, and have faith in your ability to overcome adversity and emerge stronger than ever before. God's plan is flawless and worth fighting for, so embrace the process.

CHAPTER
(Round 10)
PROCESSING FOR THE FUTURE

For a boxer, preparing for the future involves not only physical training but also mental preparation and strategic planning. In the following paragraphs, I will discuss how a boxer can approach preparing for the future.

When boxers anticipate their next fight, they often ***review their past performances*** to identify their strengths, weaknesses, and areas that need improvement. It is important for us to do the same. Reflecting on our past experiences allows us to understand what has worked well and what needs adjustment in our personal lives and endeavors.

Preparing for the future also requires ***setting clear goals.*** It is essential to define specific and measurable goals for both short-term and long-term objectives. These goals can include achieving a promotion at work, spending more quality time with family, maintaining peak physical condition, or improving certain skills in life. However, it is crucial to prioritize setting goals for our spiritual life first. This foundation will provide us with the necessary mindset and determination to succeed in the future.

Boxers typically ***create a training plan*** in collaboration with coaches and trainers. This plan encompasses physical conditioning, technical skills, and tactical strategies. It involves a combination of cardio exercises, strength training, sparring, and skill drills to enhance overall performance. Similarly, in our own lives, we can benefit from mentors who can guide us in this journey. We should seek guidance from them and spend more time in the presence of God to develop the endurance and strength needed to overcome life's challenges at every level and after every promotion.

Be sure to tend to your mental health. *Focusing on Mental Preparation* must be a part of your plan. Though I returned to Church and continued preaching and pastoring during my tough times, my focus was on the deliverance I would receive while serving. A boxer Practices visualization techniques to mentally rehearse upcoming fights and visualize success. I utilized this technique by spending time with my spiritual father, my mom, wife, and my mentor to develop mental toughness, focus, and confidence for the future.

I embraced the mindset of a boxer and followed a strict training routine, which included regular workouts, proper nutrition, and enough rest. This became even more important when I realized that I lacked certain nutrients. It is crucial to stay disciplined and stick to the training plan, even when faced with challenges or setbacks. This helps build mental strength. It also helped me devour anxiety.

By adopting the mindset of a fighter and living by principles, you can effectively prepare for the future, unlock your potential, and work towards achieving your goals. Additionally, reflecting on the past is vital for personal growth and embracing the future wholeheartedly.

SEEKING FIRST THE KINGDOM OF GOD

Through it all, you must develop a relationship with God and or recalibrate your relationship with God. Attempting to figure life out on your own can cost you so much time and sanity. You cannot live this life without the help of God. You must put all your trust and help in Him and not concern yourself with things that God is willing to do for you.

> *But seek ye first the kingdom of God, and his righteousness; and all these things shall be added unto you.*
> **Matthew 6:33**
> **KJV (King James Version)**

Seeking first the Kingdom of God is a fundamental principle taught by Jesus Christ in the New Testament. The Kingdom of God is referring to God's rule and His reign. God's existence and ability to rule and reign over all things. For this reason, whatever we need in life has already been put in place. If we seek the right source (God's Kingdom) we can have everything we need in life.

A born-again believer should prioritize God in their life. We should make a conscious decision to prioritize our relationship with God above all else. Set aside time for *prayer*, devotion, and study of the Word of God daily. In doing so, it gives us the ability to live out the will of God for our lives. Therefore, you must strive to align your thoughts, words, and actions with the principles of God's Kingdom. Seek to live a life characterized by *love*, *compassion, justice,* and *righteousness.* This is the culture of God's Kingdom and as citizens of His Kingdom we must live as the King instructs us to live.

In order to fully comprehend the revelation of the kingdom, you must be born-again, or it will not make sense and you will not be able to fully grasp all that is available in God's kingdom.

In John 3:3 Jesus is speaking to Nicodemus, a Pharisee and member of the Jewish ruling council. Jesus says to him, *"Very truly I tell you, no one can see the kingdom of God unless they are born again."* This statement by Jesus emphasizes the spiritual rebirth or transformation that is necessary for individuals to enter into a relationship with God and experience the fullness of His Kingdom. Christ teaches that this new birth is not physical but rather spiritual, involving a radical change of *heart, mind, and spirit.* To "**see the kingdom of God**" means to understand, experience, and participate in God's *reign and rule in one's life*. This verse highlights the central importance of spiritual renewal and transformation in the believer's faith, inviting individuals to turn to God in repentance, faith, and surrender to enter into a new life characterized by divine grace, love, and righteousness.

I have learned to continuously seek to grow spiritually by deepening my understanding of God's word and His ways. Not allowing my natural circumstances to dictate to me the outcome of life. Remembering the promises of God key and ultimately obeying God no matter how we feel. Purposely obeying God's commands revealed in His Word breaks heaviness, depression, and anxiety off of your life. You embrace praise instead of pouting. You learn to trust in God's wisdom and follow his leading in all areas of your life.

God has provision for you. Have faith that God will provide for your needs as you seek first His Kingdom. Trust in his promises and rely on his provision rather than worrying about material concerns. Get to know God as *Jehovah Jireh*. "**Jireh**" is a Hebrew word that means "*provider*" or "*God will provide.*" It is used in reference to God's provision. In **Genesis 22:14** (NIV), after Abraham demonstrates his faithfulness by being willing to sacrifice his son Isaac, God provides a ram in the bush for the sacrifice instead, and Abraham names the place "*The Lord Will Provide*" or "*Jehovah Jireh*" in Hebrew. This name reflects God's character as a faithful provider who meets the needs of His people.

While seeking God and waiting on His provision to manifest, actively seek opportunities to serve others and advance the Kingdom of God through acts of love, kindness, and generosity. Look for ways to use your gifts and talents to make a positive difference in the lives of others. Your future is only as bright as your service to others.

Integrate the principles of God's Kingdom into every aspect of your life, including your relationships, work, finances, business, and decision-making process. Only what you commit to the Lord will be established. Keep your focus on eternal values rather than temporary worldly concerns. Remember that seeking first the Kingdom of God is about prioritizing the things that have lasting significance and eternal value.

In context, "*all these things*" refers to the necessities of life mentioned in the preceding verses, such as food, drink, and clothing. Jesus assures those who follow Him that if they prioritize seeking God's Kingdom and living according to His righteousness, their basic needs will be provided for by God. I want to emphasize on the importance of trusting in God's provision and not being overly anxious about material concerns. As believers we must have faith in God's love, care, and kindness and to prioritize spiritual values over worldly possessions. You will save yourself a lot of heartache and worry.

In **Philippians 4:6-7** (NIV) - The apostle Paul urges believers not to be anxious about anything but to present their requests to God with thanksgiving. He promises that God's peace, which transcends all understanding, will guard their hearts and minds in Christ Jesus.

Going up to the next level in any aspect of life comes with its own set of challenges. I have realized that as I have progressed, I have encountered success that I have longed for, but I wasn't fully prepared for the battles that came my way. Whether it is in personal growth, career, ministry, or relationships, striving for greatness demands sacrifices. Remember, with every new height you reach, there are new obstacles to overcome. Yet, take heart in knowing that the power of Christ surpasses all, and even demons tremble at His name.

VICTORIOUS SCRIPTURES

These scriptures highlight the assurance of victory that believers can find in God. They inspire hope, courage, and perseverance in the face of challenges, reminding us that ultimate victory is found through faith and depending on God.

- **Psalm 18:32**: "It is God who arms me with strength and keeps my way secure." **Romans 8:37**: "Nay, in all these things we are more than conquerors through him who loved us."
- **1 Corinthians 15:57**: "But thanks be to God! He gives us the victory through our Lord Jesus Christ."
- **Philippians 4:13**: "I can do all this through him who gives me strength."
  2 Corinthians 2:14: "But thanks be to God, who always leads us as captives in Christ's triumphal procession and uses us to spread the aroma of the knowledge of him everywhere."
- **1 John 5:4**: "For everyone born of God overcomes the world. This is the victory that has overcome the world, even our faith."
- **Isaiah 41:10**: "So do not fear, for I am with you; do not be dismayed, for I am your God. I will strengthen you and help you; I will uphold you with my righteous right hand."

- **Joshua 1:9**: "Have I not commanded you? Be strong and courageous. Do not be afraid; do not be discouraged, for the Lord your God will be with you wherever you go."
- **Psalm 60:12**: "With God we will gain the victory, and he will trample down our enemies."
- **2 Timothy 4:7-8**: "I have fought the good fight, I have finished the race, I have kept the faith. Now there is in store for me the crown of righteousness, which the Lord, the righteous Judge, will award to me on that day—and not only to me, but also to all who have longed for his appearing."

Always keep in mind that you are more than a conqueror, no matter what challenges you face. There is a promise waiting for you. You will have strength even when you do not feel like you have strength. You will continue in this fight until God has finished using you to make an impact on others. By keeping your focus on Christ Jesus, victory will always be yours.

God never said that the road would be easy, or that there would not be obstacles. At times, it may feel like He has abandoned you, but that is impossible. God is faithful to His promises, including the one to never leave or forsake you. With over 7,000 promises in the Bible, choose one to hold onto each day.

If you have felt like giving up, choose to fight another day. Remember, this battle is already won and is working in your favor. Even when you are weary and feel like quitting, don't give up! If I can discover the keys to my breakthrough, so can you!

Life is a precious gift, full of secrets and wonders waiting to be uncovered. Have a heart that desires to serve God and bring Him glory through the life you have been given. He will equip you with everything you need to succeed on every front. Commit to living, learning, and growing each day. Embrace the journey of faith and trust the process. Do your best not to fight the process but process the fight!

Raise your hands in victory because in the end...

YOU ARE A WINNER!

www.ingramcontent.com/pod-product-compliance
Lightning Source LLC
Chambersburg PA
CBHW050324010526
44119CB00003B/96